The Ultimate Dessert Cookbook

Dishes, Volume 9

Olivia Bennett

Published by B&H Publishing Group, 2025.

THE ULTIMATE DESSERT COOKBOOK

First edition. February 24, 2025.

ISBN: 979-8230064084

Written by Olivia Bennett.

Table of Contents

To all the dessert lovers who find joy in every sweet bite,

To the home bakers who fill their kitchens with warmth and the scent of freshly baked treats,

And to my family and friends, whose love and encouragement have been the sweetest ingredient in this journey—

May this book bring you as much happiness as a perfectly baked cake.

Chapter 1: The Art of Dessert Making

Dessert making is both an art and a science, a craft rooted in centuries of history and cultural traditions that reflect humanity's love for sweetness and indulgence. It transcends simple sustenance, providing joy, celebration, and comfort. This chapter explores the history and cultural significance of desserts, outlines essential tools and ingredients, delves into the importance of flavor profiles, and offers practical tips for beginners and advanced bakers alike. Whether you're crafting a rustic tart or an intricate soufflé, mastering the art of dessert making is as rewarding as it is delicious.

Overview of Dessert History and Cultural Significance

Desserts, in some form, have been part of human history for thousands of years. The concept of ending a meal with something sweet is rooted in our innate preference for sugar, which provides a quick source of energy and signals ripeness and safety in nature. Over centuries, desserts have evolved from simple honey-coated nuts to elaborate creations that showcase technical skill and artistry.

The Origins of Desserts

1. Ancient Beginnings

- Honey and Fruits: The earliest desserts were natural—fruits drizzled with honey, nuts combined with syrups, or fermented drinks made from sweet fruits.

- Egyptians: The ancient Egyptians were among the first to use honey in baking, creating sweet breads and cakes.

2. Medieval Desserts

- Sugar as a Luxury: By the medieval period, sugar had become a valuable commodity. Desserts like marzipan and sugar sculptures were symbols of wealth.

- Spiced Treats: Spices like cinnamon, nutmeg, and cloves were introduced into European desserts, adding complexity to flavors.

3. Renaissance Innovations

- Pastry Making: Techniques for puff pastry and custards emerged during the Renaissance, elevating desserts into an art form.
- Chocolate and Vanilla: The arrival of cacao and vanilla from the Americas transformed desserts, leading to innovations like hot chocolate and chocolate cakes.

4. Modern Desserts

- Mass Production: The Industrial Revolution brought refined sugars, refrigeration, and mass production, making desserts more accessible.
- Artisanal Movements: Today, there is a renewed focus on small-batch, handcrafted desserts that highlight local and seasonal ingredients.

Cultural Significance

Desserts are integral to cultural traditions and celebrations worldwide:

- France: The art of pâtisserie has elevated desserts like éclairs, macarons, and mille-feuille to global fame.
- Italy: Tiramisu, panna cotta, and gelato are staples of Italian cuisine, emphasizing simple yet bold flavors.
- Middle East: Baklava, Turkish delight, and halva showcase the region's love for nuts, honey, and aromatic spices.
- Asia: Desserts like mochi, red bean cakes, and mango sticky rice highlight the use of rice, fruits, and beans in sweet treats.

The Essentials: Tools, Ingredients, and Techniques for Success

Creating desserts requires the right tools, high-quality ingredients, and foundational techniques. Each element contributes to the outcome, ensuring consistent results and delicious flavors.

Essential Tools

1. Baking Basics

- Mixing Bowls: A set of stainless steel or glass bowls in various sizes.
- Measuring Cups and Spoons: For accurate ingredient proportions.

- Spatulas and Whisks: Silicone spatulas for folding and balloon whisks for aeration.

2. Specialized Equipment

- Stand Mixer: Ideal for kneading dough, whipping cream, and mixing batters.
- Piping Bags and Tips: For decorating cakes, pastries, and cookies.
- Springform Pans: Essential for cheesecakes and other delicate desserts.
- Candy Thermometer: For precision in making caramel, syrups, or chocolate tempering.

3. Oven Essentials

- Baking Sheets: Heavy-duty sheets for even baking.
- Cooling Racks: To allow air circulation and prevent soggy bottoms.
- Silicone Mats or Parchment Paper: For nonstick surfaces.

Key Ingredients

1. Flours and Starches

- All-purpose flour for cakes and cookies.
- Almond flour for gluten-free or nutty desserts.
- Cornstarch for thickening custards and puddings.

2. Sugars and Sweeteners

- Granulated sugar for general use.
- Brown sugar for a molasses-rich flavor.
- Honey, maple syrup, or agave for natural sweetness.

3. Fats

- Butter for richness and flavor.
- Oils for moist cakes and brownies.
- Heavy cream for whipped toppings and custards.

4. Flavorings

- Vanilla beans or extract for depth.
- Cocoa powder and chocolate for richness.
- Fresh fruits, spices, and nuts for variety.

5. Leavening Agents

- Baking powder and baking soda for cakes and cookies.
- Yeast for bread-based desserts.

Mastering Techniques

1. Mixing and Folding

- Understand the difference between mixing (combining ingredients evenly) and folding (gently incorporating air for light textures).

2. Whipping and Creaming

- Whip cream to soft or stiff peaks for mousses and toppings.

- Cream butter and sugar for aerated cake batters.

3. Temperature Control

- Monitor temperatures for custards, chocolates, and caramels to avoid curdling or burning.

4. Timing

- Follow baking times closely, but always test for doneness with a skewer or toothpick.

Understanding Flavor Profiles and Balancing Sweetness, Acidity, and Texture

Great desserts balance flavors and textures to create harmony. Understanding how to manipulate sweetness, acidity, and texture ensures your desserts are never too cloying or one-dimensional.

Sweetness

- Primary source of sweetness: Sugar.

- Counteract excessive sweetness with acidic ingredients like lemon juice or berries.

Acidity

- Acidity brightens flavors and cuts through richness.

- Common acidic ingredients: Citrus fruits, yogurt, and tart fruits like raspberries.

Texture

- Contrast is key: Combine crunchy elements (like nuts or cookies) with smooth bases (like custards or mousses).
- Incorporate layers for complexity in desserts like trifles or parfaits.

Tips for Beginners and Advanced Bakers Alike

Whether you're new to dessert making or a seasoned pro, these tips can elevate your baking game.

For Beginners

1. Start Simple
   - Begin with foolproof recipes like brownies or cookies before attempting more complex desserts.
2. Follow Recipes Precisely
   - Baking is a science; measure ingredients accurately and follow instructions carefully.
3. Learn from Mistakes
   - If a cake collapses or cookies spread too much, identify the issue and try again.

For Advanced Bakers

1. Experiment with Flavors
   - Infuse creams, custards, or batters with unexpected flavors like herbs or spices.
2. Master Laminated Doughs
   - Perfect your technique for making puff pastry or croissants.
3. Focus on Presentation
   - Use plating techniques, edible garnishes, and layered textures to create visually stunning desserts.

Conclusion

The art of dessert making combines history, cultural significance, and technical skill to create something magical. By understanding the tools, ingredients, and techniques essential to this craft, as well as mastering the balance of flavors and textures, you can produce desserts that are as beautiful as they are delicious. Whether you're a beginner exploring the basics or an experienced baker pushing boundaries, dessert making offers endless opportunities for creativity and joy. So roll up your sleeves, gather your ingredients, and let the magic begin!

Chapter 2: Classic Cakes for Every Celebration

Cakes are the centerpiece of celebrations, from birthdays to weddings and everything in between. They are versatile, indulgent, and infinitely customizable, making them the perfect canvas for creative expression. This chapter explores essential cake-making techniques, offers detailed recipes for timeless classics like Vanilla Layer Cake, Chocolate Fudge Cake, Red Velvet Cake, and Lemon Drizzle Cake, and provides practical tips for decorating and adapting cakes for special occasions. Whether you're a novice baker or a seasoned pro, mastering these foundational cakes will elevate your dessert repertoire.

Essential Cake-Making Techniques: Creaming, Folding, and Baking

Mastering the art of cake-making requires understanding the fundamental techniques that create a moist, airy, and flavorful result. These techniques form the backbone of all great cakes.

1. The Creaming Method

The creaming method is one of the most common techniques used in cake-making. It creates a light, airy texture by incorporating air into the batter.

- Steps:

1. Begin with softened butter and sugar.

2. Use a stand mixer or hand mixer to beat them together until the mixture is pale and fluffy. This step traps air, which expands during baking.

3. Add eggs one at a time, beating well after each addition to ensure proper emulsification.

- Tips:

- Butter should be at room temperature but not melted.

- Scrape down the sides of the bowl frequently to ensure even mixing.

2. Folding

Folding is a gentle mixing technique used to incorporate ingredients without deflating the air in the batter.

- When to Fold:
- Incorporating whipped egg whites into a batter.
- Mixing dry ingredients into wet ingredients.
- How to Fold:

1. Use a large rubber spatula.
2. Cut through the center of the mixture, scoop around the sides, and lift the batter over itself.
3. Rotate the bowl slightly with each fold to ensure even mixing.

3. Baking Basics

The baking process is critical for achieving the perfect cake texture. Proper temperature control and timing are essential.

- Preheating: Always preheat your oven to the temperature specified in the recipe.
- Greasing and Lining Pans:
- Grease pans with butter or cooking spray, then line the bottom with parchment paper to prevent sticking.
- Filling the Pan:
- Fill pans two-thirds full to allow room for the batter to rise.
- Testing for Doneness:
- Insert a toothpick into the center of the cake. If it comes out clean or with a few moist crumbs, the cake is done.

Recipes: Vanilla Layer Cake, Chocolate Fudge Cake, Red Velvet Cake, and Lemon Drizzle Cake

Each of these classic cake recipes serves as a foundation for countless variations and is beloved for its universal appeal.

1. Vanilla Layer Cake

A timeless classic, vanilla layer cake is versatile and perfect for any celebration.

- Ingredients:
- 2 1/2 cups all-purpose flour
- 2 1/2 teaspoons baking powder
- 1/2 teaspoon salt
- 3/4 cup unsalted butter, softened
- 2 cups granulated sugar
- 4 large eggs
- 1 teaspoon vanilla extract
- 1 cup whole milk
- Instructions:

1. Preheat the oven to 350°F (175°C). Grease and line two 8-inch round cake pans.
2. Whisk together flour, baking powder, and salt in a bowl.
3. In a separate bowl, cream butter and sugar until light and fluffy. Add eggs one at a time, then mix in vanilla.
4. Gradually add the dry ingredients, alternating with milk, beginning and ending with the dry ingredients.
5. Divide the batter evenly between the pans and bake for 30–35 minutes. Cool completely before frosting.

2. Chocolate Fudge Cake

Rich and indulgent, this cake is a chocolate lover's dream.

- Ingredients:
- 1 3/4 cups all-purpose flour
- 1 1/2 teaspoons baking powder
- 1/2 teaspoon baking soda
- 3/4 cup unsweetened cocoa powder
- 2 cups granulated sugar
- 1 cup buttermilk
- 1/2 cup vegetable oil
- 2 large eggs
- 1 teaspoon vanilla extract

- 1 cup hot coffee
- Instructions:

1. Preheat the oven to 350°F (175°C). Grease and line two 9-inch round pans.
2. Sift together flour, baking powder, baking soda, cocoa powder, and sugar.
3. In a separate bowl, whisk buttermilk, oil, eggs, and vanilla.
4. Add wet ingredients to the dry mixture, then stir in hot coffee.
5. Divide batter evenly and bake for 30–35 minutes. Cool before assembling.

3. Red Velvet Cake

This vibrant cake is iconic for its tangy flavor and striking red color.

- Ingredients:
- 2 1/2 cups all-purpose flour
- 1 teaspoon baking powder
- 1 teaspoon baking soda
- 1/4 cup cocoa powder
- 1 teaspoon salt
- 1 cup buttermilk
- 1 teaspoon white vinegar
- 1 1/2 cups granulated sugar
- 3/4 cup vegetable oil
- 2 large eggs
- 1 teaspoon vanilla extract
- 2 tablespoons red food coloring
- Instructions:

1. Preheat the oven to 350°F (175°C). Grease and line two 8-inch round pans.
2. Whisk together flour, baking powder, baking soda, cocoa powder, and salt.
3. In a separate bowl, mix buttermilk, vinegar, sugar, oil, eggs, vanilla, and food coloring.
4. Gradually mix wet ingredients into dry ingredients.

5. Bake for 25–30 minutes. Cool completely before frosting with cream cheese frosting.

4. Lemon Drizzle Cake

Bright and zesty, this cake is perfect for spring and summer gatherings.

- Ingredients:
- 1 3/4 cups all-purpose flour
- 1 1/2 teaspoons baking powder
- 1/4 teaspoon salt
- 3/4 cup unsalted butter, softened
- 1 cup granulated sugar
- 3 large eggs
- Zest of 2 lemons
- 1/3 cup lemon juice
- 1/2 cup whole milk
- Instructions:

1. Preheat the oven to 350°F (175°C). Grease and line a loaf pan.
2. Whisk together flour, baking powder, and salt.
3. Cream butter and sugar until light and fluffy. Add eggs one at a time, then mix in lemon zest and juice.
4. Alternate adding dry ingredients and milk, beginning and ending with dry ingredients.
5. Bake for 40–45 minutes. Drizzle with lemon glaze while warm.

Decorating Basics: Frosting, Piping, and Finishing Touches

Decorating transforms a simple cake into a stunning centerpiece. Here are essential techniques:

Frosting

1. Types of Frosting:
   - Buttercream: Smooth, creamy, and versatile.

- Cream Cheese Frosting: Tangy and perfect for Red Velvet or carrot cakes.
- Ganache: Luxurious and glossy, made with chocolate and cream.

2. Tips for Frosting:

- Apply a crumb coat (a thin layer of frosting) to seal in crumbs before the final layer.
- Use an offset spatula for even spreading.

Piping

- Use piping bags with decorative tips to create borders, rosettes, or intricate designs.
- Practice on parchment paper before decorating the cake.

Finishing Touches

- Edible Decorations: Sprinkles, fruit, edible flowers, or chocolate shavings.
- Drizzles: Add a dramatic effect with caramel, ganache, or fruit coulis.
- Personalized Messages: Use melted chocolate or icing to write messages.

How to Adapt Classic Recipes for Special Occasions

Classic cakes can be customized to suit any celebration:

- Birthdays: Add vibrant frosting colors or sprinkles to a Vanilla Layer Cake.
- Weddings: Stack tiers of Red Velvet Cake with white cream cheese frosting.
- Holidays: Infuse a Chocolate Fudge Cake with peppermint extract for Christmas.
- Spring Events: Decorate Lemon Drizzle Cake with fresh berries or edible flowers.

Conclusion

Classic cakes are timeless for a reason: they are versatile, delicious, and adaptable to any occasion. By mastering essential techniques, experimenting with iconic recipes, and honing your decorating skills, you can create cakes that are as visually stunning as they are delicious. Whether you're baking a simple Lemon Drizzle Cake for an intimate gathering or a multi-layered showstopper for a wedding, the joy of crafting these cakes lies in their ability to bring people together in celebration.

Chapter 3: Decadent Chocolate Desserts

Chocolate is the epitome of indulgence in the dessert world, offering a rich, velvety flavor that is both versatile and irresistible. From its complex chemistry to its luxurious texture, chocolate plays a starring role in some of the most beloved desserts. In this chapter, we'll dive into the science of working with chocolate, explore recipes for classics like Molten Lava Cakes, Chocolate Mousse, Chocolate Truffles, and Fudge Brownies, examine the nuances of dark, milk, and white chocolate, and share tips for achieving perfect textures and richness in your chocolate creations.

The Science of Working with Chocolate

To master chocolate desserts, you must first understand the unique properties of chocolate and how to handle it effectively. Whether melting, tempering, or pairing it with other ingredients, the science of chocolate is both fascinating and crucial to your success.

Melting Chocolate

Melting chocolate may seem simple, but achieving smooth, glossy results requires attention to detail.

1. Use High-Quality Chocolate

- Choose chocolate with a high cocoa butter content (typically 60% or more for dark chocolate).

- Avoid chocolate chips for melting, as they often contain stabilizers that prevent proper melting.

2. Avoid Overheating

- Chocolate is delicate and can burn if heated too quickly. Melt it slowly over low heat.

3. Melting Methods

- Double Boiler: Place chopped chocolate in a heatproof bowl over a pot of simmering water. Stir gently until melted.

- Microwave: Heat chocolate in 20-second intervals, stirring after each, to prevent scorching.

4. Keep Water Away

- Even a small amount of water can cause chocolate to seize (become grainy and lumpy). Always dry your tools thoroughly.

Tempering Chocolate

Tempering chocolate ensures a glossy finish and crisp snap, essential for professional-looking desserts like truffles or chocolate decorations.

1. What Is Tempering?

- Tempering stabilizes cocoa butter crystals, giving chocolate its shiny appearance and smooth texture.

2. Tempering Process

- Melt chocolate to 110°F–115°F (43°C–46°C).

- Cool it to 80°F (27°C) by stirring or adding finely chopped tempered chocolate.

- Reheat gently to 88°F–90°F (31°C–32°C) for dark chocolate (or slightly lower for milk and white chocolate).

3. Uses for Tempered Chocolate

- Dipping fruits, coating truffles, or creating decorations like curls or shards.

Pairing Chocolate

Chocolate pairs beautifully with a wide range of flavors. Understanding these pairings allows you to create complex and memorable desserts.

1. Fruits

- Dark chocolate complements tart fruits like raspberries, cherries, and oranges.

- Milk chocolate pairs well with sweeter fruits like bananas and strawberries.

2. Nuts

- Hazelnuts, almonds, and pecans add crunch and balance chocolate's richness.

3. Spices

- Cinnamon, cardamom, and chili enhance chocolate's warmth.

4. Liquors and Coffee

- Espresso deepens chocolate's flavor, while liquors like rum, Grand Marnier, or Kahlúa add complexity.

Recipes: Molten Lava Cakes, Chocolate Mousse, Chocolate Truffles, and Fudge Brownies

Now that you understand how to handle chocolate, let's explore recipes for some decadent chocolate desserts.

1. Molten Lava Cakes

Molten lava cakes are known for their rich, gooey centers, making them a showstopper at any dinner party.

- Ingredients:
- 4 ounces dark chocolate (70%)
- 1/2 cup unsalted butter
- 1 cup powdered sugar
- 2 large eggs
- 2 large egg yolks
- 1/4 cup all-purpose flour
- Pinch of salt
- Instructions:

1. Preheat the oven to 425°F (220°C). Grease and dust four ramekins with cocoa powder.
2. Melt chocolate and butter in a double boiler. Cool slightly.
3. Whisk eggs, egg yolks, and powdered sugar until thick and pale.
4. Fold in the melted chocolate mixture, then sift in flour and salt. Mix until smooth.
5. Divide batter evenly among ramekins. Bake for 12–14 minutes, or until the edges are set but the centers are soft.
6. Let cool slightly before inverting onto plates. Serve immediately.

2. Chocolate Mousse

This light, airy dessert showcases chocolate's luxurious texture.

- Ingredients:
- 6 ounces dark chocolate
- 3 large eggs, separated
- 1/4 cup granulated sugar
- 1 cup heavy cream
- 1 teaspoon vanilla extract
- Instructions:

1. Melt chocolate in a double boiler and let cool slightly.
2. Whisk egg yolks into the melted chocolate.
3. Beat egg whites to soft peaks, gradually adding sugar until stiff peaks form.
4. In a separate bowl, whip heavy cream with vanilla until soft peaks form.
5. Fold whipped cream into the chocolate mixture, then gently fold in egg whites.
6. Spoon into serving dishes and chill for at least 2 hours before serving.

3. Chocolate Truffles

These bite-sized delights are perfect for gifting or an elegant dessert platter.

- Ingredients:
- 8 ounces dark chocolate
- 1/2 cup heavy cream
- 1 tablespoon unsalted butter
- Cocoa powder, chopped nuts, or shredded coconut for coating
- Instructions:

1. Heat cream and butter in a saucepan until just simmering.
2. Pour over chopped chocolate and let sit for 5 minutes. Stir until smooth.
3. Chill the mixture for 1–2 hours until firm.
4. Scoop small amounts and roll into balls. Coat with cocoa powder, nuts, or coconut.

4. Fudge Brownies

Fudge brownies are a classic dessert, balancing dense, chewy texture with rich chocolate flavor.

- Ingredients:

- 1/2 cup unsalted butter
- 1 cup granulated sugar
- 2 large eggs
- 1 teaspoon vanilla extract
- 1/3 cup cocoa powder
- 1/2 cup all-purpose flour
- 1/4 teaspoon salt
- 1/4 teaspoon baking powder
- Instructions:

1. Preheat oven to 350°F (175°C). Grease an 8x8-inch baking pan.
2. Melt butter in a saucepan. Remove from heat and stir in sugar, eggs, and vanilla.
3. Mix in cocoa powder, flour, salt, and baking powder.
4. Spread batter evenly in the pan and bake for 20–25 minutes. Let cool before slicing.

Exploring Dark, Milk, and White Chocolate in Desserts

Each type of chocolate brings unique flavors and characteristics to desserts. Knowing when and how to use them is key.

Dark Chocolate

- Flavor: Intense and bittersweet, with notes of coffee or fruit.
  - Uses: Ideal for truffles, mousses, and lava cakes due to its bold flavor.

Milk Chocolate

- Flavor: Sweeter and creamier with a smooth finish.
  - Uses: Great for brownies, cookies, and frostings.

White Chocolate

- Flavor: Sweet and vanilla-forward.

- Uses: Perfect for ganaches, glazes, or paired with fruits like berries or citrus.

Tips for Achieving the Perfect Texture and Richness

1. Use Room-Temperature Ingredients
   - Cold ingredients can cause chocolate mixtures to seize.
2. Don't Skimp on Quality
   - High-quality chocolate enhances both flavor and texture.
3. Incorporate Air Gently
   - Fold whipped cream or egg whites carefully to maintain a light texture.
4. Experiment with Add-Ins
   - Mix in nuts, spices, or fruit for added complexity.
5. Chill Properly
   - Allow desserts like mousse or truffles to set fully in the refrigerator.

Conclusion

Decadent chocolate desserts are a testament to the versatility and allure of chocolate. By understanding the science behind chocolate, mastering essential techniques, and experimenting with classic recipes, you can create showstopping treats that cater to every occasion and palate. Whether crafting a gooey lava cake, a silky mousse, or indulgent truffles, the journey into the world of chocolate is as rewarding as the desserts themselves. Let your creativity shine, and indulge in the art of chocolate-making!

Chapter 4: Fruit-Based Desserts: Light and Refreshing

Fruit-based desserts hold a special place in the world of confections. Their natural sweetness, vibrant colors, and refreshing flavors make them the perfect choice for everything from casual meals to elegant gatherings. Whether you're working with juicy summer berries, tart citrus fruits, or the comforting flavors of stone fruits, understanding how to harness the full potential of fresh produce is key to crafting delicious desserts. This chapter explores how to make the most of seasonal fruits, offers detailed recipes for classics like Berry Pavlova, Lemon Bars, Fruit Tarts, and Peach Cobbler, and provides techniques for balancing sweetness and acidity as well as preserving fruit flavors in jams and compotes.

Making the Most of Seasonal Fruits in Desserts

Seasonal fruits are at the heart of many desserts, offering superior flavor and texture compared to their out-of-season counterparts. Here's how to choose, prepare, and showcase fruits in your creations.

1. Choosing the Best Fruits

- Seasonal Advantage: Fruits harvested during their natural growing season are fresher, more flavorful, and often more affordable.
- Ripeness Matters: Look for fruits that are fully ripe but not overripe. For example, peaches should be fragrant and slightly soft to the touch, while berries should be plump and brightly colored.
- Local Produce: Farmers' markets and local orchards often provide the freshest options, supporting both quality and sustainability.

2. Preparing Fruits for Desserts

- Washing: Always rinse fruits thoroughly to remove dirt and pesticides. For delicate berries, rinse gently in a colander.
- Peeling and Pitting: Use a paring knife or peeler for smooth-skinned fruits like peaches. For cherries and plums, a pitting tool is invaluable.

- Slicing and Dicing: Uniform cuts ensure even cooking and presentation. A mandoline slicer is helpful for thin slices.

3. Enhancing Fruit Flavors

- Maceration: Toss fruits with sugar or a splash of liqueur to draw out their juices and intensify their flavor.

- Roasting or Grilling: These methods caramelize the natural sugars in fruits, adding depth and complexity.

- Zesting: Citrus zest adds brightness and aromatic intensity to fruit-based desserts.

Recipes: Berry Pavlova, Lemon Bars, Fruit Tarts, and Peach Cobbler

Below are step-by-step guides to creating some of the most beloved fruit-based desserts.

1. Berry Pavlova

Pavlova is a light and airy dessert that pairs crisp meringue with whipped cream and fresh berries.

- Ingredients:
- 4 large egg whites
- 1 cup granulated sugar
- 1 teaspoon cornstarch
- 1 teaspoon white vinegar
- 1 teaspoon vanilla extract
- 1 cup heavy cream
- 2 tablespoons powdered sugar
- 2 cups mixed berries (strawberries, blueberries, raspberries)
- Instructions:

1. Preheat oven to 250°F (120°C). Line a baking sheet with parchment paper.

2. Beat egg whites until soft peaks form. Gradually add sugar, beating until glossy stiff peaks form.

3. Fold in cornstarch, vinegar, and vanilla. Spoon meringue onto the baking sheet, shaping into a round with a slight dip in the center.

4. Bake for 1 hour, then turn off the oven and let the meringue cool inside.

5. Whip heavy cream with powdered sugar until soft peaks form. Top the meringue with whipped cream and fresh berries.

2. Lemon Bars

Lemon bars are a perfect balance of tart lemon filling and buttery shortbread crust.

- Ingredients:
-For the crus:
- 1 cup unsalted butter, softened
- 1/2 cup powdered sugar
- 2 cups all-purpose flour
- For the filling:
- 4 large eggs
- 1 1/2 cups granulated sugar
- 1/4 cup all-purpose flour
- 1/2 cup fresh lemon juice
- Zest of 2 lemons
- Instructions:

1. Preheat oven to 350°F (175°C). Line a 9x13-inch baking pan with parchment paper.

2. Mix crust ingredients until crumbly, then press into the pan. Bake for 20 minutes or until lightly golden.

3. Whisk eggs, sugar, flour, lemon juice, and zest until smooth. Pour over the crust and bake for 20–25 minutes.

4. Cool completely before cutting into squares. Dust with powdered sugar.

3. Fruit Tarts

Fruit tarts combine a buttery crust, creamy filling, and fresh fruit for a visually stunning dessert.

- Ingredients:
- For the crust:

- 1 1/2 cups all-purpose flour
- 1/2 cup unsalted butter, cold
- 1/4 cup powdered sugar
- For the filling:
- 1 1/2 cups whole milk
- 1/3 cup granulated sugar
- 2 tablespoons cornstarch
- 4 large egg yolks
- 1 teaspoon vanilla extract
- For topping:
- Sliced fresh fruit (kiwi, berries, mango)
- Optional: Apricot glaze
- Instructions:

1. Preheat oven to 350°F (175°C). Blend crust ingredients until dough forms. Press into a tart pan and bake for 15 minutes.
2. Heat milk and sugar in a saucepan. In a bowl, whisk egg yolks and cornstarch. Gradually add warm milk to the eggs, then return to the saucepan and cook until thickened. Stir in vanilla.
3. Spread filling in the cooled crust. Arrange fruit on top and brush with apricot glaze for shine.

4. Peach Cobbler

Peach cobbler is a comforting dessert with a juicy filling and golden biscuit topping.

- Ingredients:
- For the filling:
- 6 ripe peaches, peeled and sliced
- 1/2 cup granulated sugar
- 1 teaspoon cinnamon
- For the topping:
- 1 cup all-purpose flour
- 1/4 cup granulated sugar
- 1 teaspoon baking powder
- 1/2 cup cold butter, cubed

- 1/4 cup whole milk
- Instructions:

1. Preheat oven to 375°F (190°C). Toss peaches with sugar and cinnamon and spread in a baking dish.
2. Mix flour, sugar, and baking powder. Cut in butter until crumbly, then stir in milk to form dough.
3. Drop spoonfuls of dough over peaches. Bake for 30–35 minutes or until topping is golden.

Balancing Sweetness and Acidity with Fresh Produce

The best fruit-based desserts strike a perfect balance between sweetness and acidity, enhancing the natural flavors of the fruit.

1. Enhance Sweetness

- Use a touch of sugar, honey, or maple syrup to amplify fruit flavors without overpowering them.
- Ripe fruits often need minimal additional sweetness.

2. Brighten with Acidity

- Add lemon juice, lime juice, or vinegar to balance sweetness, especially in jams and cobblers.
- Acidity also prevents fruits like apples and bananas from browning.

3. Balance is Key

- For tart fruits like rhubarb or cranberries, pair with sweeter elements like vanilla custard or a buttery crust.
- For sweet fruits like mangoes or bananas, add a tart element such as passion fruit or citrus zest.

Techniques for Preserving Fruit Flavors in Jams and Compotes

Preserving fruits extends their shelf life and captures their peak flavor for use in desserts year-round.

Jams

Jams are thickened fruit preserves made by cooking fruit with sugar and sometimes pectin.

- Basic Recipe: Combine equal parts fruit and sugar. Simmer until thickened and store in sterilized jars.
- Flavor Variations: Add vanilla, spices, or citrus zest for depth.

Compotes

Compotes are chunky fruit sauces that pair beautifully with cakes, ice creams, or yogurts.

- Basic Recipe: Cook chopped fruit with sugar and a splash of water or juice until soft but still textured.
- Uses: Spoon over pancakes, mix into trifles, or swirl into cheesecakes.

Conclusion

Fruit-based desserts celebrate the natural beauty and flavor of seasonal produce, offering a refreshing and versatile option for any occasion. By mastering the art of selecting, preparing, and enhancing fruits, you can create vibrant desserts that delight the senses. From the airy elegance of Berry Pavlova to the comforting warmth of Peach Cobbler, these recipes and techniques ensure that every fruit-filled creation is as delicious as it is memorable. Let the flavors of nature guide your creativity and bring a touch of brightness to your dessert repertoire.

Chapter 5: Pies and Tarts: A Flaky Affair

Pies and tarts hold an esteemed place in the world of baking, offering a delightful combination of flaky crusts and flavorful fillings. These versatile desserts can range from simple, rustic creations to elegant, polished masterpieces. In this chapter, we'll delve into the art of mastering pie crusts, explore recipes for classics like Apple Pie, Lemon Meringue Tart, Pecan Pie, and Chocolate Ganache Tart, share tips for achieving the perfect golden crust, and introduce savory twists for adventurous bakers.

Mastering Pie Crusts: Shortcrust, Puff, and Graham Cracker

A well-made crust is the foundation of any great pie or tart. Understanding the characteristics of different crusts and mastering their techniques will elevate your creations.

1. Shortcrust Pastry

Shortcrust pastry is the classic choice for most pies and tarts, offering a tender, buttery texture.

- Key Characteristics:
- Crisp and crumbly, yet sturdy enough to hold fillings.
- Perfect for fruit pies, custard tarts, and savory quiches.
- Ingredients:
- 2 1/2 cups all-purpose flour
- 1 cup unsalted butter, chilled and cubed
- 1/4 cup granulated sugar (optional, for sweet crusts)
- 1/2 teaspoon salt
- 4–6 tablespoons ice water
- Method:

1. Combine flour, sugar (if using), and salt in a bowl.
2. Cut in butter using a pastry cutter or your fingertips until the mixture resembles coarse crumbs.

3. Gradually add ice water, one tablespoon at a time, until the dough comes together.

4. Shape into a disc, wrap in plastic wrap, and chill for at least 30 minutes before rolling.

2. Puff Pastry

Puff pastry is a laminated dough known for its light, flaky layers.

- Key Characteristics:
- Buttery and flaky, with a golden finish.
- Ideal for elegant tarts and turnovers.
- Ingredients:
- 2 1/2 cups all-purpose flour
- 1 teaspoon salt
- 1 cup unsalted butter, chilled
- 1/2 cup ice water
- Method:

1. Mix flour and salt in a bowl. Cut in half the butter until it resembles coarse crumbs.

2. Add water gradually to form a dough. Chill for 30 minutes.

3. Roll out dough, dot with remaining butter, and fold into thirds. Chill for 30 minutes.

4. Repeat the rolling and folding process three more times to create layers.

3. Graham Cracker Crust

This no-roll crust is a quick and easy option, especially for chilled pies.

- Key Characteristics:
- Sweet and crumbly, with a slightly nutty flavor.
- Perfect for cheesecakes, key lime pie, and ganache tarts.
- Ingredients:
- 1 1/2 cups graham cracker crumbs
- 1/3 cup granulated sugar
- 6 tablespoons unsalted butter, melted
- Method:

1. Mix graham cracker crumbs, sugar, and melted butter until combined.

2. Press firmly into a pie dish or tart pan, covering the bottom and sides.

3. Bake at 350°F (175°C) for 8–10 minutes if using a baked filling, or chill for no-bake pies.

Recipes: Apple Pie, Lemon Meringue Tart, Pecan Pie, and Chocolate Ganache Tart

These classic recipes showcase the versatility of pies and tarts, blending traditional techniques with indulgent flavors.

1. Apple Pie

A quintessential dessert, apple pie combines tender apples with a buttery, flaky crust.

- Ingredients:

-For the crus:

- 2 1/2 cups all-purpose flour
- 1 teaspoon salt
- 1 cup unsalted butter, chilled and cubed
- 6 tablespoons ice water

-For the filling:

- 6 medium apples (Granny Smith or Honeycrisp), peeled and sliced
- 3/4 cup granulated sugar
- 2 tablespoons all-purpose flour
- 1 teaspoon cinnamon
- 1/4 teaspoon nutmeg
- 1 tablespoon lemon juice
- 2 tablespoons unsalted butter, cut into small pieces

- Instructions:

1. Prepare the crust using the shortcrust pastry method. Divide into two discs and chill.

2. Toss apples with sugar, flour, cinnamon, nutmeg, and lemon juice.

3. Roll out one disc of dough and fit into a 9-inch pie dish. Add the apple filling and dot with butter.

4. Roll out the second disc of dough and place over the filling. Seal edges and cut slits for steam to escape.

5. Bake at 375°F (190°C) for 50–60 minutes until golden brown.

2. Lemon Meringue Tart

This tart pairs tangy lemon curd with a sweet, fluffy meringue topping.

- Ingredients:
- For the crust: Use shortcrust pastry.
- For the lemon filling:
- 1 cup granulated sugar
- 1/4 cup cornstarch
- 1/4 teaspoon salt
- 1 1/2 cups water
- 3 large egg yolks
- 1/2 cup fresh lemon juice
- 2 tablespoons unsalted butter
- For the meringue:
- 3 large egg whites
- 1/4 teaspoon cream of tartar
- 6 tablespoons granulated sugar
- Instructions:

1. Blind bake the crust until golden and set aside.

2. Combine sugar, cornstarch, and salt in a saucepan. Gradually whisk in water and cook over medium heat until thickened.

3. Temper egg yolks with the hot mixture, then return to the saucepan. Stir in lemon juice and butter.

4. Pour lemon filling into the crust. Whip egg whites with cream of tartar, gradually adding sugar, until stiff peaks form. Spread over the filling.

5. Bake at 350°F (175°C) for 10–12 minutes until meringue is golden.

3. Pecan Pie

This rich, nutty pie is a Southern favorite.

- Ingredients:
- For the crust: Use shortcrust pastry.

- For the filling:
- 1 cup light corn syrup
- 1 cup granulated sugar
- 3 large eggs
- 1/4 cup unsalted butter, melted
- 1 teaspoon vanilla extract
- 1 1/2 cups pecan halves
- Instructions:

1. Preheat oven to 350°F (175°C). Fit crust into a pie dish and set aside.
2. Whisk together corn syrup, sugar, eggs, melted butter, and vanilla. Stir in pecans.
3. Pour filling into the crust and bake for 50–60 minutes until set. Cool before serving.

4. Chocolate Ganache Tart

A decadent dessert for chocolate lovers.

- Ingredients:
- For the crust: Use graham cracker crust.
- For the filling:
- 8 ounces dark chocolate, chopped
- 1 cup heavy cream
- 1 teaspoon vanilla extract
- Optional toppings: Fresh berries, whipped cream, or sea salt
- Instructions:

1. Prepare and bake the graham cracker crust.
2. Heat cream until just simmering and pour over chopped chocolate. Let sit for 5 minutes, then stir until smooth.
3. Stir in vanilla and pour ganache into the crust. Chill for at least 2 hours. Decorate as desired.

Tips for Achieving the Perfect Golden Crust

1. Keep Ingredients Cold

- Chilled butter and water prevent gluten development, resulting in a tender crust.

2. Don't Overwork the Dough

- Handle the dough minimally to avoid toughness.

3. Blind Baking

- For custard or cream pies, bake the crust partially before adding the filling to prevent sogginess.

4. Egg Wash

- Brush the crust with a beaten egg for a glossy, golden finish.

5. Use Pie Weights

- Prevent puffing during blind baking by using weights or dried beans.

Savory Twists for Adventurous Bakers

Pies and tarts aren't just for desserts! Savory variations offer equally satisfying results.

- Quiche Lorraine: A rich custard filling with bacon, cheese, and onions in a shortcrust pastry.
- Tomato Tart: Puff pastry topped with heirloom tomatoes, fresh herbs, and goat cheese.
- Chicken Pot Pie: A creamy filling of chicken and vegetables topped with a flaky crust.
- Mushroom and Gruyere Tart: Earthy mushrooms paired with creamy Gruyere in a buttery tart shell.

Conclusion

Pies and tarts are timeless desserts that balance the art of a perfectly flaky crust with the creativity of diverse fillings. By mastering techniques for shortcrust, puff pastry, and graham cracker crusts, and experimenting with both sweet and savory recipes, you'll unlock endless possibilities in your baking journey. From the rustic charm of an apple pie to the elegant simplicity of a chocolate ganache tart, these creations are sure to delight and impress for any occasion. Let your imagination run wild, and enjoy the flaky affair!

Chapter 6: Frozen Treats: Ice Creams, Sorbets, and Beyond

Frozen treats, from ice creams and sorbets to popsicles and frozen yogurt, are universally loved for their refreshing textures and flavors. They offer endless possibilities for creativity, catering to a wide range of tastes and occasions. This chapter explores the science behind freezing, provides detailed recipes for Vanilla Bean Ice Cream, Raspberry Sorbet, and Frozen Yogurt, teaches how to craft no-churn ice creams, and introduces ice cream sandwiches and popsicles as fun and versatile desserts.

The Science of Freezing: Achieving Creamy Textures

Creating frozen treats with the perfect creamy or smooth texture involves understanding the science behind freezing. The goal is to minimize ice crystal formation while maintaining a balance of air, fat, and sugar.

1. The Role of Ice Crystals

- What Happens During Freezing: As water freezes, it forms ice crystals. Large crystals result in a gritty texture, while small crystals create a smooth mouthfeel.

- How to Minimize Ice Crystals:

- Churn While Freezing: Churning incorporates air and breaks up ice crystals.

- Use Stabilizers: Ingredients like egg yolks, cornstarch, or xanthan gum help control water distribution.

2. Balancing Fat, Sugar, and Air

- Fat: Provides richness and a creamy texture. Common sources include cream, milk, and egg yolks.

- Sugar: Lowers the freezing point, keeping the mixture soft and scoopable. Alternatives like honey or corn syrup can also add complexity.

- Air: Incorporated during churning, air lightens the texture and prevents dense, icy results.

3. Temperature and Equipment

- Freezer Temperature: Set your freezer to 0°F (-18°C) for optimal storage and freezing.
- Ice Cream Makers: Machines churn while freezing, creating a consistent texture.
- No-Churn Methods: Use whipped cream or condensed milk to replicate air incorporation without a machine.

Recipes: Vanilla Bean Ice Cream, Raspberry Sorbet, and Frozen Yogurt

These classic recipes showcase the versatility of frozen treats, from creamy ice creams to refreshing sorbets and tangy yogurts.

1. Vanilla Bean Ice Cream

This timeless classic is the perfect base for endless variations or delicious on its own.

- Ingredients:
- 2 cups heavy cream
- 1 cup whole milk
- 3/4 cup granulated sugar
- 1 vanilla bean (or 1 tablespoon vanilla extract)
- 4 large egg yolks
- Instructions:

1. Heat cream, milk, and sugar in a saucepan over medium heat. Split the vanilla bean, scrape the seeds, and add both seeds and pod to the mixture. Heat until steaming (do not boil).
2. Whisk egg yolks in a separate bowl. Gradually add the hot cream mixture to the yolks, whisking constantly to temper.
3. Return the mixture to the saucepan and cook over low heat, stirring constantly, until it thickens enough to coat the back of a spoon.

4. Strain through a fine-mesh sieve and chill for at least 4 hours.

5. Churn in an ice cream maker according to manufacturer instructions. Freeze for 2–4 hours before serving.

2. Raspberry Sorbet

Light and refreshing, sorbet is a dairy-free alternative to ice cream, perfect for fruit lovers.

- Ingredients:
- 4 cups fresh or frozen raspberries
- 3/4 cup granulated sugar
- 1/2 cup water
- 1 tablespoon lemon juice
- Instructions:

1. Blend raspberries until smooth, then strain through a fine-mesh sieve to remove seeds.
2. Heat sugar and water in a saucepan until dissolved. Cool to room temperature.
3. Combine the raspberry puree, sugar syrup, and lemon juice. Chill the mixture for 2 hours.
4. Churn in an ice cream maker or pour into a shallow dish and freeze, stirring every 30 minutes until smooth.

3. Frozen Yogurt

Frozen yogurt offers a tangy, creamy alternative to traditional ice cream, with endless flavor possibilities.

- Ingredients:
- 2 cups full-fat Greek yogurt
- 3/4 cup granulated sugar
- 1 teaspoon vanilla extract
- Optional mix-ins: fruit purees, chocolate chips, or nuts
- Instructions:

1. Whisk yogurt, sugar, and vanilla extract until smooth. Chill for 1–2 hours.

2. Churn in an ice cream maker, adding mix-ins during the last few minutes of churning.

3. Freeze until firm and serve.

Crafting No-Churn Ice Creams for Easy Indulgence

No-churn ice cream is a game-changer for those who want homemade frozen treats without special equipment. The base relies on whipped cream and sweetened condensed milk to achieve a creamy texture.

Basic No-Churn Recipe

- Ingredients:
  - 2 cups heavy cream
  - 1 can (14 ounces) sweetened condensed milk
  - 1 teaspoon vanilla extract
  - Instructions:

1. Whip heavy cream to stiff peaks in a large bowl.

2. Fold in sweetened condensed milk and vanilla extract gently, maintaining the airiness.

3. Pour into a freezer-safe container, cover, and freeze for at least 6 hours or overnight.

Flavor Variations

1. Chocolate Swirl: Add ribbons of melted chocolate or fudge sauce.

2. Peanut Butter Cup: Mix in chunks of peanut butter cups and swirl with peanut butter.

3. Strawberry Shortcake: Fold in crushed shortbread cookies and a swirl of strawberry puree.

Ice Cream Sandwiches and Popsicles for All Ages

Frozen treats like ice cream sandwiches and popsicles are fun, versatile, and universally appealing.

1. Ice Cream Sandwiches

- Building the Perfect Sandwich:
    - Use soft, chewy cookies or brownies to hold the ice cream.
    - Soften ice cream slightly before spreading between cookies to avoid breakage.
    - Roll edges in sprinkles, crushed nuts, or mini chocolate chips for added texture.
    - Recipe: Classic Chocolate Chip Ice Cream Sandwiches:

    1. Bake large, soft chocolate chip cookies.
    2. Spread softened vanilla ice cream onto one cookie and top with another.
    3. Wrap in parchment paper and freeze until firm.

2. Popsicles

Popsicles are a nostalgic treat that's easy to make with just a few ingredients and a mold.

- Recipe: Creamy Mango Popsicles:
- Blend 2 cups fresh mango chunks with 1 cup coconut milk and 2 tablespoons honey.
- Pour into popsicle molds, insert sticks, and freeze for 4–6 hours.
- Recipe: Chocolate Fudge Popsicles:
- Combine 2 cups whole milk, 1/3 cup cocoa powder, 1/2 cup sugar, and 1/2 teaspoon vanilla extract. Heat until sugar dissolves, cool, and pour into molds.

Tips for Success with Frozen Treats

1. Chill Everything: Keep bowls, whisks, and ingredients cold for better results.
2. Don't Overfill Molds: Leave space for expansion when freezing popsicles.
3. Serve at the Right Temperature: Let ice cream sit at room temperature for 5–10 minutes before scooping for the best texture.
4. Experiment with Mix-Ins: Add nuts, cookie chunks, or fruit for texture and flavor variety.

Conclusion

Frozen treats bring joy to every occasion, offering a refreshing escape and a canvas for creativity. By understanding the science of freezing, experimenting with classic recipes, and exploring the ease of no-churn methods, you can craft a variety of desserts to delight any palate. From creamy vanilla ice cream to tangy raspberry sorbet and playful popsicles, these recipes and techniques will transform your kitchen into a haven of icy indulgence. Let your imagination run wild, and enjoy the endless possibilities of frozen desserts!

Chapter 7: Cookies and Bars for Every Occasion

Cookies and bars are the quintessential treat for any occasion, from casual snacks to elegant dessert platters. They are versatile, easy to make, and endlessly customizable to suit a wide range of tastes and preferences. Whether you prefer cookies that are soft and chewy, crisp and buttery, or a bit of both, mastering a few essential techniques and recipes will ensure consistent, delicious results every time. In this chapter, we will explore the science of cookie textures, detailed recipes for classics like Chocolate Chip Cookies, Oatmeal Raisin Bars, Macarons, and Biscotti, and tips for shaping, baking, and storing cookies. We'll also delve into creative variations for holiday and seasonal themes.

Essential Techniques for Perfect Cookies

Creating the perfect cookie begins with understanding how ingredients, techniques, and baking times influence texture and flavor. Whether you want a cookie that's chewy, crispy, or soft, a few simple adjustments can make all the difference.

1. Chewy Cookies

Chewy cookies are dense, moist, and satisfying, often characterized by a slightly underbaked center.

- Key Factors:

- High Moisture Content: Use ingredients like brown sugar and melted butter to add moisture.

- Short Baking Time: Bake until just set to prevent over-drying.

- Chilling the Dough: Refrigerating the dough helps control spread and intensifies flavor.

2. Crispy Cookies

Crispy cookies are thin and crunchy, with a satisfying snap.

- Key Factors:

- High Sugar Content: Granulated sugar helps cookies spread and crisp during baking.

- Lower Moisture: Use less butter and skip chilling the dough.

- Longer Baking Time: Bake until golden brown for a crisp texture.

3. Soft Cookies

Soft cookies are tender and cake-like, often with a fluffy interior.

- Key Factors:

- Use More Flour: A higher flour-to-fat ratio creates a sturdier structure.

- Incorporate Eggs: Eggs add moisture and structure, contributing to softness.

- Short Baking Time: Remove cookies from the oven as soon as they are set.

4. Mixing Methods

- Creaming: Beating butter and sugar until light and fluffy incorporates air for softer cookies.

- Melting Butter: Melted butter results in denser, chewier cookies.

- Folding: Gently fold in mix-ins like chocolate chips or nuts to avoid overmixing.

5. Shaping Techniques

- Scoop and Drop: Use a cookie scoop for uniform cookies that bake evenly.

- Rolling and Cutting: For sugar cookies or shortbread, roll dough to an even thickness before cutting.

- Piping: For delicate cookies like macarons, use a piping bag to shape.

Recipes: Chocolate Chip Cookies, Oatmeal Raisin Bars, Macarons, and Biscotti

These classic recipes showcase the versatility and appeal of cookies and bars.

1. Chocolate Chip Cookies

A timeless favorite, these cookies strike the perfect balance between chewy and crispy.

- Ingredients:
- 2 1/4 cups all-purpose flour
- 1 teaspoon baking soda
- 1 teaspoon salt
- 1 cup unsalted butter, softened
- 3/4 cup granulated sugar
- 3/4 cup brown sugar
- 1 teaspoon vanilla extract
- 2 large eggs
- 2 cups semisweet chocolate chips
- Instructions:

1. Preheat the oven to 375°F (190°C). Line baking sheets with parchment paper.
2. Whisk flour, baking soda, and salt in a bowl.
3. Cream butter, granulated sugar, brown sugar, and vanilla until light and fluffy. Add eggs one at a time.
4. Gradually mix in dry ingredients. Fold in chocolate chips.
5. Drop rounded tablespoons of dough onto the prepared sheets. Bake for 9–11 minutes. Cool on wire racks.

2. Oatmeal Raisin Bars

These hearty bars are packed with oats, raisins, and a touch of cinnamon, making them perfect for snacks or desserts.

- Ingredients:
- 1 1/2 cups old-fashioned oats
- 1 cup all-purpose flour
- 1 teaspoon cinnamon
- 1/2 teaspoon baking soda
- 1/2 teaspoon salt
- 1/2 cup unsalted butter, melted
- 1/2 cup brown sugar

- 1/4 cup granulated sugar
- 1 large egg
- 1 teaspoon vanilla extract
- 3/4 cup raisins
- Instructions:

1. Preheat oven to 350°F (175°C). Grease a 9x9-inch baking pan.
2. Mix oats, flour, cinnamon, baking soda, and salt.
3. Combine melted butter, sugars, egg, and vanilla. Stir into dry ingredients. Fold in raisins.
4. Press dough evenly into the pan. Bake for 20–25 minutes. Cool before slicing.

3. Macarons

These delicate French cookies are crisp on the outside and chewy on the inside, with a flavorful filling.

- Ingredients:
- For the shells:
- 1 3/4 cups powdered sugar
- 1 cup almond flour
- 3 large egg whites, at room temperature
- 1/4 cup granulated sugar
- Gel food coloring (optional)
- For the filling:
- 1/2 cup buttercream, ganache, or jam
- Instructions:

1. Sift powdered sugar and almond flour together. Set aside.
2. Beat egg whites until foamy. Gradually add granulated sugar and beat to stiff peaks. Add food coloring if desired.
3. Fold dry ingredients into the meringue until the batter flows like lava.
4. Pipe small circles onto a lined baking sheet. Tap the sheet to release air bubbles. Let sit for 30–60 minutes to form a skin.
5. Bake at 300°F (150°C) for 15–18 minutes. Cool completely before filling.

4. Biscotti

These twice-baked cookies are crunchy and perfect for dunking in coffee or tea.

- Ingredients:
- 2 cups all-purpose flour
- 1 teaspoon baking powder
- 1/4 teaspoon salt
- 1/2 cup granulated sugar
- 1/2 cup brown sugar
- 2 large eggs
- 1 teaspoon vanilla extract
- 1 cup chopped almonds or chocolate chips
- Instructions:

1. Preheat oven to 350°F (175°C). Line a baking sheet with parchment paper.
2. Whisk flour, baking powder, and salt.
3. Beat sugars and eggs until pale. Add vanilla, then mix in dry ingredients and almonds.
4. Shape dough into a log and bake for 25 minutes. Cool slightly, then slice into 1/2-inch pieces.
5. Arrange slices cut-side down and bake for 10 minutes per side.

Tips for Shaping, Baking, and Storing Cookies

1. Shaping:
   - Chill dough for cleaner cuts and reduced spreading.
   - Use cookie cutters for festive shapes.
2. Baking:
   - Bake one sheet at a time in the center of the oven for even results.
   - Rotate the pan halfway through baking to ensure uniform browning.
3. Storing:
   - Store cookies in an airtight container at room temperature for up to a week.
   - Freeze unbaked dough or baked cookies for longer storage.

Variations for Holiday and Seasonal Themes

Cookies and bars are easy to adapt for any holiday or season. Here are some ideas:

1. Christmas:

- Gingerbread Cookies: Add molasses and spices for a festive twist.
- Peppermint Bark Bars: Layer crushed candy canes over chocolate.

2. Easter:

- Lemon Sugar Cookies: Add lemon zest and glaze for a springtime flavor.
- Carrot Cake Bars: Incorporate shredded carrots, spices, and cream cheese frosting.

3. Fall:

- Pumpkin Chocolate Chip Cookies: Replace some butter with pumpkin puree and add warm spices.
- Apple Cinnamon Bars: Mix diced apples and cinnamon into a bar base.

4. Summer:

- S'mores Bars: Layer graham crackers, chocolate, and marshmallows in a bar pan.
- Berry Thumbprint Cookies: Fill cookie centers with fresh berry jam.

Conclusion

Cookies and bars are beloved for their simplicity, versatility, and ability to adapt to any occasion. By mastering the techniques for achieving different textures, experimenting with classic recipes, and incorporating seasonal variations, you can create treats that delight family, friends, and guests alike. Whether you're crafting macarons for an elegant tea party, baking oatmeal bars for an after-school snack, or decorating festive cookies for the holidays, these timeless creations will bring joy and satisfaction to every bite. Let your creativity shine and enjoy the art of cookie baking!

Chapter 8: Pastries and Croissants: Layers of Perfection

Pastries and croissants are the epitome of indulgence, showcasing the magic of buttery, flaky layers that melt in your mouth. These baked goods are the result of meticulous techniques, attention to detail, and a touch of patience. In this chapter, we'll explore the art of creating laminated dough, dive into recipes for Classic Croissants, Danish Pastries, Éclairs, and Cream Puffs, and discuss filling and glazing techniques to achieve professional-quality results. Additionally, we'll share time-saving hacks for home bakers who want to enjoy these treats without investing hours in the kitchen.

The Art of Laminated Dough: Puff Pastry and Croissant Dough

Laminated dough is the foundation of many pastries, including croissants, Danish pastries, and puff pastry-based creations. This technique involves layering butter and dough through a series of folds and rolls, creating the signature flaky texture.

1. Puff Pastry

Puff pastry is an unleavened dough known for its delicate, buttery layers. It relies solely on steam and the layering process to achieve its rise and flakiness.

- Characteristics:
- Flaky, light, and crisp texture.
- Used in both sweet and savory applications, such as tarts, turnovers, and palmiers.
- Ingredients:
- 2 1/2 cups all-purpose flour
- 1 teaspoon salt
- 1 cup unsalted butter, cold and cubed
- 1/2 cup cold water

- Method:

1. Mix flour and salt, then cut in half the butter until the mixture resembles coarse crumbs.

2. Add cold water gradually to form a dough. Chill for 30 minutes.

3. Roll out dough, place remaining butter in the center, and fold the dough over it like an envelope.

4. Roll out and fold into thirds. Repeat this process four more times, chilling the dough between folds.

2. Croissant Dough

Croissant dough is similar to puff pastry but incorporates yeast for additional rise and a tender, airy texture.

- Characteristics:
- Buttery, flaky layers with a slightly chewy interior.
- Ideal for breakfast pastries or sandwiches.
- Ingredients:
- 4 cups all-purpose flour
- 1/4 cup granulated sugar
- 2 teaspoons salt
- 2 1/4 teaspoons active dry yeast
- 1 cup whole milk, warm
- 1 cup unsalted butter, cold and cubed
- Method:

1. Activate yeast in warm milk. Mix flour, sugar, and salt in a bowl, then add the yeast mixture.

2. Knead the dough until smooth. Chill for 1 hour.

3. Roll out dough, place butter in the center, and fold like an envelope. Chill for 30 minutes.

4. Roll and fold the dough into thirds. Repeat this process three more times, chilling between folds.

Recipes: Classic Croissants, Danish Pastries, Éclairs, and Cream Puffs

Once you've mastered laminated dough, you can create a wide range of pastries. Here are some classic recipes to get started.

1. Classic Croissants

Flaky and buttery, croissants are a bakery staple.

- Ingredients:
- Croissant dough (see above)
- 1 egg, beaten (for egg wash)
- Instructions:

1. Roll out chilled croissant dough into a rectangle. Cut into triangles.
2. Starting at the wide end, roll each triangle into a crescent shape.
3. Place croissants on a baking sheet lined with parchment paper. Cover and proof until doubled in size (about 1–2 hours).
4. Brush with egg wash and bake at 375°F (190°C) for 15–20 minutes until golden brown.

2. Danish Pastries

Danish pastries are versatile, featuring a variety of fillings and shapes.

- Ingredients:
- Croissant dough
- Fruit preserves, cream cheese, or almond paste (for filling)
- 1 egg, beaten (for egg wash)
- Instructions:

1. Roll out dough and cut into squares. Add a dollop of filling to the center of each square.
2. Fold corners toward the center or create other shapes like twists or pinwheels.
3. Proof until puffy. Brush with egg wash and bake at 375°F (190°C) for 15–20 minutes.

3. Éclairs

Éclairs are made from choux pastry, filled with cream, and topped with a glossy glaze.

- Ingredients:
- *For the choux pastry*:
- 1 cup water
- 1/2 cup unsalted butter
- 1 cup all-purpose flour
- 4 large eggs
- For the filling:
- 2 cups pastry cream or whipped cream
- For the glaze:
- 1/2 cup chocolate ganache
- Instructions:

1. Preheat oven to 375°F (190°C). Heat water and butter in a saucepan until boiling. Stir in flour until a smooth dough forms.
2. Remove from heat and let cool slightly. Beat in eggs one at a time until smooth and glossy.
3. Pipe into 4-inch strips on a baking sheet. Bake for 25–30 minutes.
4. Cool completely, then fill with pastry cream and top with chocolate ganache.

4. Cream Puffs

These airy pastries are filled with sweet or savory fillings.

- Ingredients:
- Choux pastry (see above)
- Sweetened whipped cream or pastry cream (for filling)
- Powdered sugar (for dusting)
- Instructions:

1. Pipe choux pastry into small rounds on a baking sheet. Bake at 375°F (190°C) for 20–25 minutes.
2. Cool completely, then slice in half and fill with cream. Dust with powdered sugar.

Filling and Glazing Techniques for Professional Results

The right fillings and glazes can transform a simple pastry into a gourmet creation.

Filling Techniques

1. Piping:

- Use a piping bag fitted with a round tip for precision.
- Fill éclairs and cream puffs from the bottom or side to avoid disturbing their appearance.

2. Layering:

- Spread fillings like almond cream or custard between layers of laminated dough for Danishes.

3. Mixing Flavors:

- Combine complementary flavors like chocolate and orange, or vanilla and berries, for depth.

Glazing Techniques

1. Chocolate Ganache:

- Combine equal parts chopped chocolate and hot cream. Stir until smooth, then drizzle or dip pastries.

2. Icing Sugar Glaze:

- Mix powdered sugar with milk or lemon juice until thick but pourable. Use for Danish pastries or scones.

3. Egg Wash:

- Brush pastries with beaten egg before baking for a shiny, golden finish.

Time-Saving Hacks for Home Bakers

While traditional laminated dough can be time-consuming, these hacks help streamline the process without sacrificing quality.

1. Store-Bought Puff Pastry

- High-quality frozen puff pastry is a convenient alternative for recipes like turnovers, tarts, and palmiers.

- Thaw according to package instructions and handle gently to preserve the layers.

2. Overnight Chilling

- Prepare dough the night before and chill it overnight to break up the workload.

- Proofing in the refrigerator also enhances flavor development.

3. Shortcut Croissants

- Use pre-made dough sheets or crescent roll dough for quick croissants. While not as authentic, they offer a similar experience with minimal effort.

4. Simplified Danish Shapes

- Instead of intricate folds, use a muffin tin to create easy Danish cups. Press dough into the tin, fill, and bake.

Conclusion

Pastries and croissants are a labor of love, but the results are worth the effort. Mastering the art of laminated dough opens the door to a world of buttery, flaky delights, while learning classic recipes like croissants, Danish pastries, éclairs, and cream puffs ensures you're prepared to impress any crowd. With professional filling and glazing techniques and time-saving hacks, even the busiest home bakers can enjoy the magic of these creations. So roll up your sleeves, embrace the layers, and experience the joy of pastry perfection!

Chapter 9: Custards, Puddings, and Creamy Delights

Custards, puddings, and creamy desserts epitomize indulgence, offering velvety textures and rich flavors that delight the palate. These desserts rely on the transformative power of eggs, dairy, and sugar, along with precise techniques to achieve their characteristic smoothness and stability. In this chapter, we'll explore the science behind creamy desserts, share recipes for classics like Crème Brûlée, Chocolate Pudding, Vanilla Custard, and Banana Pudding, and delve into essential techniques like tempering and setting custards. To inspire your creativity, we'll also provide innovative spins on traditional recipes.

Understanding the Role of Eggs and Dairy in Creamy Desserts

Eggs and dairy are the cornerstones of custards and puddings. Their unique properties contribute to the texture, flavor, and structure of these desserts.

1. Eggs: The Foundation of Custards

Eggs play a dual role as a thickening agent and structural support.

- Egg Yolks:

- Rich in fats and proteins, egg yolks create a smooth, velvety texture.

- They stabilize emulsions, binding fat and water in the mixture.

- Egg Whites:

- Contain proteins that help custards set. When whipped, they introduce air, adding lightness to certain recipes (e.g., soufflés).

- Coagulation:

- Heat causes egg proteins to unfold and bond, thickening the custard.

- Precise temperature control prevents overcooking, which can result in curdling.

2. Dairy: Creaminess and Flavor

Dairy adds richness, moisture, and a creamy texture.

- Milk:
- The primary liquid in many custards, milk ensures a smooth consistency.
- Whole milk is preferred for its balance of fat and water.
- Cream:
- Increases the fat content, adding a luxurious mouthfeel.
- Heavy cream is often used in richer desserts like Crème Brûlée.
- Evaporated and Condensed Milk:
- Common in puddings for their concentrated flavor and sweetness.

3. Sugar: Sweetness and Stability

Sugar not only sweetens but also affects texture by interfering with protein coagulation, preventing curdling.

- Granulated Sugar:
- The most common sweetener in custards and puddings.
- Brown Sugar and Molasses:
- Add depth and a caramelized flavor.
- Honey and Maple Syrup:
- Provide natural sweetness and a distinctive taste.

Recipes: Crème Brûlée, Chocolate Pudding, Vanilla Custard, and Banana Pudding

Master these classic recipes to understand the fundamental techniques of creamy dessert making.

1. Crème Brûlée

This elegant dessert features a creamy custard base with a caramelized sugar crust.

- Ingredients:
- 2 cups heavy cream
- 1 vanilla bean (or 1 teaspoon vanilla extract)
- 5 large egg yolks

- 1/2 cup granulated sugar
- Additional sugar for the caramelized topping
- Instructions:

1. Preheat the oven to 325°F (160°C). Place ramekins in a deep baking dish.
2. Heat cream and the split vanilla bean (or extract) in a saucepan until steaming. Remove from heat and let steep.
3. Whisk egg yolks and sugar until pale. Gradually temper the warm cream into the yolk mixture.
4. Strain the custard into the ramekins. Pour hot water into the baking dish to reach halfway up the sides of the ramekins.
5. Bake for 35–40 minutes, until the custard is set but slightly jiggly in the center. Cool, then chill for at least 2 hours.
6. Sprinkle sugar over the top and caramelize with a kitchen torch or broiler.

2. Chocolate Pudding

This classic dessert combines deep chocolate flavor with a creamy texture.

- Ingredients:
- 1/3 cup granulated sugar
- 2 tablespoons unsweetened cocoa powder
- 2 tablespoons cornstarch
- 1/8 teaspoon salt
- 2 3/4 cups whole milk
- 1/2 cup semisweet chocolate chips
- 1 teaspoon vanilla extract
- Instructions:

1. Whisk sugar, cocoa powder, cornstarch, and salt in a saucepan.
2. Gradually add milk, whisking to combine. Cook over medium heat, stirring constantly, until thickened and bubbling.
3. Remove from heat and stir in chocolate chips and vanilla until smooth.
4. Pour into serving dishes and chill for at least 2 hours.

3. Vanilla Custard

A versatile base, vanilla custard can be served on its own or used in trifles and tarts.

- Ingredients:
- 2 cups whole milk
- 1/2 cup granulated sugar
- 3 large egg yolks
- 2 tablespoons cornstarch
- 1 teaspoon vanilla extract
- Instructions:

1. Heat milk in a saucepan until steaming. Whisk sugar, egg yolks, and cornstarch in a bowl until smooth.
2. Temper the warm milk into the egg mixture, then return to the saucepan.
3. Cook over low heat, stirring constantly, until thickened. Remove from heat and stir in vanilla.
4. Strain the custard and chill before serving.

4. Banana Pudding

This Southern favorite layers creamy pudding with bananas and vanilla wafers.

- Ingredients:
- 2 cups whole milk
- 1/2 cup granulated sugar
- 3 tablespoons cornstarch
- 3 large egg yolks
- 2 teaspoons vanilla extract
- 3–4 ripe bananas
- 1 box vanilla wafers
- Whipped cream (optional)
- Instructions:

1. Heat milk in a saucepan until steaming. Whisk sugar, cornstarch, and egg yolks in a bowl.
2. Temper the milk into the egg mixture, then return to the saucepan. Cook until thickened, then stir in vanilla.

3. Layer pudding, sliced bananas, and vanilla wafers in a dish. Repeat layers and top with whipped cream if desired.

4. Chill for at least 2 hours before serving.

Techniques for Tempering and Setting Custards

Mastering tempering and setting is crucial for creamy desserts that are smooth and free of lumps.

1. Tempering

Tempering prevents eggs from curdling when exposed to heat.

- How to Temper:

1. Slowly add hot liquid to the eggs while whisking constantly.

2. Return the mixture to the saucepan and continue cooking over low heat.

- Tip: Always use a fine mesh sieve to remove any curdled bits.

2. Setting Custards

Custards set through gentle heat, either on the stovetop or in the oven.

- Stovetop Custards:

- Cook over medium-low heat, stirring constantly, until the mixture thickens enough to coat the back of a spoon.

- Baked Custards:

- Bake custards like Crème Brûlée in a water bath to ensure even cooking and prevent cracks.

- Chilling:

- Allow custards to cool completely before refrigerating, which helps them firm up.

Creative Spins on Traditional Recipes

Elevate classic recipes with innovative flavors and techniques.

1. Salted Caramel Crème Brûlée

- Add a swirl of salted caramel to the custard base before baking for a sweet-salty twist.

2. Mocha Chocolate Pudding

- Mix in 1 tablespoon of instant coffee granules for a sophisticated mocha flavor.

3. Coconut Vanilla Custard

- Substitute coconut milk for regular milk and garnish with toasted coconut flakes.

4. Peanut Butter Banana Pudding

- Add a layer of peanut butter whipped cream for a rich, nutty flavor.

5. Seasonal Variations

- Use seasonal fruits or spices to adapt recipes. For example:

- Add pumpkin puree and cinnamon to Vanilla Custard for a fall-inspired dessert.

- Infuse milk with lavender or rosemary for a floral or herbaceous twist.

Conclusion

Custards, puddings, and creamy desserts are timeless indulgences that rely on simple ingredients and precise techniques. By mastering the roles of eggs and dairy, tempering and setting methods, and classic recipes, you can create smooth, luscious desserts that impress every time. Whether sticking to traditional favorites or experimenting with creative variations, these creamy delights are sure to become staples in your repertoire. Embrace the art of custard-making and enjoy the endless possibilities of these decadent treats.

Chapter 10: Cheesecakes and No-Bake Wonders

Cheesecakes are universally loved for their rich, creamy texture and versatility. Whether baked to perfection or chilled as a no-bake treat, they provide a blank canvas for a variety of flavors and toppings. This chapter explores the art of mastering cheesecake, delves into recipes for New York Cheesecake, Oreo Cheesecake, Lemon Cheesecake, and No-Bake Strawberry Cheesecake, and offers tips for creating perfect crusts, achieving smooth fillings, and avoiding cracks. With these techniques and recipes, you'll be able to craft flawless cheesecakes for any occasion.

Mastering the Cheesecake: Baked vs. No-Bake Varieties

Understanding the differences between baked and no-bake cheesecakes is essential to choosing the right method for your dessert.

1. Baked Cheesecakes

Baked cheesecakes rely on eggs to achieve their firm yet creamy texture. The filling is typically cooked in a water bath to prevent cracks and ensure even baking.

- Characteristics:
- Dense and rich texture.
- Smooth and creamy when properly baked.
- Best for traditional flavors like New York Cheesecake.
- Pros:
- Classic texture and flavor.
- Stands up well to heavy toppings or layering.
- Cons:
- Requires careful attention to prevent overbaking and cracking.
- More time-intensive due to baking and cooling.

2. No-Bake Cheesecakes

No-bake cheesecakes are set using gelatin, whipped cream, or cream cheese, eliminating the need for an oven.

- Characteristics:
- Lighter, mousse-like texture.
- Requires refrigeration to set.
- Ideal for fresh fruit flavors or quick desserts.
- Pros:
- Easier and quicker to prepare.
- No risk of cracking.
- Cons:
- May be less stable than baked cheesecakes.
- Requires precise refrigeration for proper setting.

Creating Perfect Crusts and Smooth Fillings

A great cheesecake starts with a well-balanced crust and a perfectly smooth filling. Here's how to achieve both.

1. The Perfect Crust

- Types of Crusts:
  - Graham Cracker Crust: The most popular choice for its buttery, sweet flavor.
  - Cookie Crust: Made with crushed Oreos or digestive biscuits for a richer base.
  - Nut-Based Crust: Adds crunch and complements flavors like chocolate or caramel.
  - Basic Recipe for Graham Cracker Crust:
  - 1 1/2 cups graham cracker crumbs
  - 1/4 cup granulated sugar
  - 6 tablespoons unsalted butter, melted
  - Instructions:

1. Mix the crumbs, sugar, and melted butter until evenly combined.

2. Press the mixture firmly into the bottom (and slightly up the sides) of a springform pan.

3. Bake at 350°F (175°C) for 8–10 minutes for baked cheesecakes, or chill for no-bake varieties.

2. Achieving Smooth Fillings

- Ingredients:
  - Always use room-temperature cream cheese to ensure a smooth texture.
  - Use heavy cream or sour cream for added richness and moisture.
  - Mixing Tips:
  - Beat cream cheese and sugar until completely smooth before adding other ingredients.
  - Add eggs one at a time for even incorporation.
  - Avoid overmixing to prevent incorporating too much air, which can cause cracks during baking.

Recipes: New York Cheesecake, Oreo Cheesecake, Lemon Cheesecake, and No-Bake Strawberry Cheesecake

Here are detailed recipes for both baked and no-bake cheesecakes.

1. New York Cheesecake

This classic cheesecake is rich, dense, and velvety.

- Ingredients:
- For the crust:
- 1 1/2 cups graham cracker crumbs
- 6 tablespoons unsalted butter, melted
- For the filling:
- 4 (8-ounce) packages cream cheese, room temperature
- 1 1/4 cups granulated sugar
- 4 large eggs
- 1 cup sour cream
- 2 teaspoons vanilla extract

- Instructions:

1. Preheat oven to 325°F (160°C). Prepare the crust and press into a springform pan.

2. Beat cream cheese and sugar until smooth. Add eggs one at a time, then mix in sour cream and vanilla.

3. Pour filling over the crust. Bake in a water bath for 60–70 minutes, or until the edges are set and the center is slightly jiggly.

4. Turn off the oven and leave the cheesecake inside with the door cracked for 1 hour. Cool completely, then chill for at least 4 hours before serving.

2. Oreo Cheesecake

A decadent dessert featuring an Oreo crust and filling studded with cookies.

- Ingredients:
- For the crust:
- 24 Oreo cookies, finely crushed
- 6 tablespoons unsalted butter, melted
- For the filling:
- 3 (8-ounce) packages cream cheese, room temperature
- 3/4 cup granulated sugar
- 3 large eggs
- 1 cup sour cream
- 1 teaspoon vanilla extract
- 10–12 crushed Oreo cookies
- Instructions:

1. Preheat oven to 325°F (160°C). Prepare the crust using crushed Oreos and press into a springform pan.

2. Beat cream cheese and sugar until smooth. Add eggs one at a time, then mix in sour cream and vanilla.

3. Fold in crushed Oreos. Pour filling over the crust.

4. Bake in a water bath for 55–65 minutes. Cool and chill before serving. Garnish with whipped cream and Oreos.

3. Lemon Cheesecake

This bright and tangy cheesecake is perfect for spring and summer.

- Ingredients:
- For the crust:
- 1 1/2 cups digestive biscuit crumbs
- 6 tablespoons unsalted butter, melted
- For the filling:
- 3 (8-ounce) packages cream cheese, room temperature
- 1 cup granulated sugar
- 3 large eggs
- 1/2 cup sour cream
- 1/4 cup fresh lemon juice
- Zest of 2 lemons
- Instructions:

1. Preheat oven to 325°F (160°C). Prepare the crust and press into a springform pan.
2. Beat cream cheese and sugar until smooth. Add eggs one at a time, then mix in sour cream, lemon juice, and zest.
3. Pour filling over the crust. Bake in a water bath for 60–70 minutes. Cool and chill before serving. Garnish with whipped cream and lemon slices.

4. No-Bake Strawberry Cheesecake

A quick and easy dessert with a light, mousse-like texture.

- Ingredients:
- For the crust:
- 1 1/2 cups graham cracker crumbs
- 6 tablespoons unsalted butter, melted
- For the filling:
- 2 (8-ounce) packages cream cheese, room temperature
- 1 cup powdered sugar
- 1 teaspoon vanilla extract
- 1 1/2 cups heavy cream, whipped to stiff peaks

- 1 cup strawberry puree
- For the topping:
- Fresh strawberries, halved
- Instructions:

1. Prepare the crust and press into a springform pan. Chill while preparing the filling.
2. Beat cream cheese, powdered sugar, and vanilla until smooth. Fold in whipped cream and strawberry puree.
3. Pour filling over the crust and smooth the top. Chill for at least 6 hours or overnight.
4. Garnish with fresh strawberries before serving.

Tips for Avoiding Cracks and Achieving Flawless Presentation

Cracks are a common issue in baked cheesecakes, but they can be avoided with proper techniques.

1. Preventing Cracks

- Use a Water Bath:
    - The steam from a water bath ensures even cooking and prevents the surface from drying out.
- Avoid Overbaking:
    - Remove the cheesecake from the oven when the center is still slightly jiggly. It will continue to set as it cools.
- Cool Gradually:
    - Sudden temperature changes can cause cracks. Allow the cheesecake to cool slowly in the oven before transferring to the counter.

2. Perfect Presentation

- Smoothing the Top:
    - Use an offset spatula to create a smooth surface before baking.
- Garnishes:
    - Add whipped cream, fresh fruit, or chocolate curls for a polished look.

- Serving Clean Slices:
- Wipe the knife with a damp cloth between cuts for neat slices.

Conclusion

Cheesecakes and no-bake wonders are versatile desserts that can be tailored to any occasion. By mastering the differences between baked and no-bake varieties, perfecting crusts and fillings, and following expert tips to avoid cracks, you'll be able to create stunning cheesecakes every time. Whether you're serving a classic New York Cheesecake, a crowd-pleasing Oreo Cheesecake, a tangy Lemon Cheesecake, or a refreshing No-Bake Strawberry Cheesecake, these recipes and techniques will ensure your desserts are as beautiful as they are delicious.

Chapter 11: Global Desserts: A World of Sweetness

Desserts are a universal language of indulgence, and each culture has its unique take on satisfying the human craving for sweetness. From the rich creaminess of Italy's Tiramisu to the delicate chewiness of Japan's Mochi, the flaky Baklava of the Middle East, and Spain's crispy, sugar-coated Churros, global desserts tell stories of tradition, innovation, and celebration. This chapter explores the cultural roots of iconic international desserts, provides recipes for recreating them at home, offers tips for adapting traditional recipes for modern kitchens, and delves into the art of layering and flavor balancing in global treats.

Exploring International Desserts and Their Cultural Roots

Desserts are deeply rooted in the history and traditions of their countries of origin, often reflecting local ingredients, religious practices, and festive customs.

1. Tiramisu (Italy)

Tiramisu, meaning "pick me up," is a decadent Italian dessert made with layers of espresso-soaked ladyfingers, mascarpone cream, and cocoa. Originating in the Veneto region, it is a modern classic that gained widespread popularity in the 20th century.

- Cultural Significance:
- Served at celebrations and family gatherings.
- Reflects Italy's love for coffee and creamy textures.

2. Mochi (Japan)

Mochi is a chewy rice cake made from glutinous rice, traditionally prepared for Japanese New Year (Oshogatsu) but now enjoyed year-round in various forms, including filled mochi (daifuku) and ice cream mochi.

- Cultural Significance:
- Symbolizes good fortune and longevity.
- Often shared during festivals and special occasions.

3. Baklava (Middle East)

Baklava is a rich, layered pastry made with phyllo dough, nuts, and honey or syrup. Its origins are contested, with Turkey, Greece, and other Middle Eastern countries claiming it as their own. Regardless, it is a hallmark of hospitality and celebration.

- Cultural Significance:
- Commonly served during holidays like Ramadan and Easter.
- Represents the art of hospitality and sharing.

4. Churros (Spain)

Churros are fried dough pastries, crispy on the outside and tender on the inside, often coated in sugar and cinnamon. They are typically enjoyed as a breakfast or snack, accompanied by hot chocolate for dipping.

- Cultural Significance:
- A staple of Spanish street food culture.
- Also popular during festivals and fairs.

Recipes: Tiramisu, Mochi, Baklava, and Churros

Recreate these iconic desserts in your own kitchen with step-by-step recipes.

1. Tiramisu (Italy)

- Ingredients:
  - 1 cup brewed espresso, cooled
  - 2 tablespoons coffee liqueur (optional)
  - 6 large egg yolks
  - 3/4 cup granulated sugar
  - 16 ounces mascarpone cheese
  - 1 1/2 cups heavy cream, whipped to soft peaks
  - 24–30 ladyfingers

- Unsweetened cocoa powder for dusting
- Instructions:

1. Mix espresso and coffee liqueur in a shallow dish. Set aside.
2. Whisk egg yolks and sugar in a heatproof bowl over simmering water until thick and pale. Remove from heat and cool slightly.
3. Fold mascarpone into the yolk mixture. Gently fold in whipped cream.
4. Dip ladyfingers briefly in the espresso mixture and layer them in a dish.
5. Spread half the mascarpone mixture over the ladyfingers. Repeat with another layer.
6. Chill for at least 4 hours. Dust with cocoa powder before serving.

2. Mochi (Japan)

- Ingredients:
    - 1 cup glutinous rice flour (mochiko)
    - 3/4 cup water
    - 1/4 cup granulated sugar
    - Potato starch for dusting
    - Optional fillings: sweetened red bean paste, ice cream
    - Instructions:

1. Mix rice flour, water, and sugar in a microwave-safe bowl until smooth.
2. Microwave for 1 minute. Stir, then microwave in 30-second intervals until the mixture is thick and sticky.
3. Dust a clean surface with potato starch. Transfer the mochi and roll it out.
4. Cut into circles and fill with red bean paste or ice cream. Pinch the edges to seal.
5. Chill before serving.

3. Baklava (Middle East)

- Ingredients:
    - 1 package phyllo dough, thawed
    - 2 cups mixed nuts (walnuts, pistachios, almonds), finely chopped
    - 1 cup unsalted butter, melted
    - 1/2 cup granulated sugar

- 1 teaspoon ground cinnamon
- *For the syrup*:
- 1 cup water
- 1 cup sugar
- 1/2 cup honey
- 1 teaspoon lemon juice
- Instructions:

1. Preheat oven to 350°F (175°C). Grease a 9x13-inch baking dish.
2. Layer half the phyllo sheets in the dish, brushing each layer with melted butter.
3. Mix nuts, sugar, and cinnamon. Spread over the phyllo layers.
4. Layer the remaining phyllo sheets, brushing each with butter. Cut into diamond shapes.
5. Bake for 40–50 minutes. Meanwhile, prepare the syrup by boiling water, sugar, honey, and lemon juice until thickened.
6. Pour syrup over the hot baklava. Cool before serving.

4. Churros (Spain)

- Ingredients:
  - 1 cup water
  - 2 tablespoons granulated sugar
  - 1/2 teaspoon salt
  - 2 tablespoons unsalted butter
  - 1 cup all-purpose flour
  - 2 large eggs
  - Vegetable oil for frying
  - Sugar and cinnamon for coating
  - Instructions:

1. Heat water, sugar, salt, and butter in a saucepan until boiling. Remove from heat and stir in flour until a dough forms.
2. Beat in eggs one at a time until smooth.
3. Heat oil in a deep pan. Pipe dough into the hot oil using a star-tipped piping bag. Fry until golden.

4. Toss churros in a mixture of sugar and cinnamon. Serve with hot chocolate or caramel sauce.

Adapting Traditional Recipes for Modern Kitchens

While these desserts have historical roots, modern techniques and tools can simplify their preparation.

- Tiramisu:
- Use store-bought ladyfingers and an electric mixer for the mascarpone mixture.
- Substitute coffee liqueur with non-alcoholic vanilla extract for a family-friendly version.
- Mochi:
- Microwave the dough instead of steaming it traditionally.
- Use pre-made ice cream balls for easy filling.
- Baklava:
- Replace phyllo dough with puff pastry for a quicker version.
- Experiment with different nuts, such as pecans or hazelnuts.
- Churros:
- Use an air fryer for a lighter, healthier option.
- Add flavored extracts (like orange or vanilla) to the dough for a unique twist.

The Art of Layering and Flavor Balancing in Global Treats

Layering and flavor balancing are key to creating sophisticated desserts that showcase the complexity of international cuisines.

1. Layering

- Visual Appeal:
- Use transparent dishes to highlight layers in desserts like tiramisu or trifles.
- Texture Contrast:

- Combine crunchy elements (e.g., nuts or biscuits) with creamy or chewy components.

- Flavor Development:

- Alternate sweet, tart, and rich layers to create depth.

2. Flavor Balancing

- Sweetness:

- Pair with acidic or bitter elements (e.g., coffee in tiramisu or lemon in baklava syrup).

- Spices:

- Add warmth with cinnamon, nutmeg, or cardamom, common in baklava and churros.

- Umami:

- Use ingredients like matcha in mochi for an earthy balance to sweetness.

Conclusion

Global desserts offer a journey into the culinary traditions and flavors of different cultures. By mastering recipes for iconic treats like Tiramisu, Mochi, Baklava, and Churros, and adapting them for modern kitchens, you can recreate these world-renowned delights with ease. Embrace the art of layering and flavor balancing to elevate your creations, making each dessert not just a treat, but a celebration of global sweetness. Let your kitchen become an international stage where tradition meets innovation, and every bite tells a story.

Chapter 12: Elegant Plated Desserts for Entertaining

Plated desserts are the crown jewel of fine dining, offering a harmonious blend of flavors, textures, and visual appeal. These desserts are more than just food—they're an experience that elevates the dining occasion. Whether you're hosting an intimate dinner or a grand event, mastering restaurant-quality plated desserts can impress and delight your guests. In this chapter, we'll cover the techniques for creating stunning plated desserts, provide recipes for Poached Pears, Mille-Feuille, Chocolate Fondant, and Lemon Soufflé, explore the use of garnishes and sauces to elevate presentation, and share strategies for time management when preparing multiple components.

Techniques for Creating Restaurant-Quality Plated Desserts

Achieving a polished and professional look for your plated desserts requires precision, creativity, and a good understanding of the key techniques.

1. Balancing Flavors and Textures

- Contrast: Pair creamy elements with crunchy components, or balance sweetness with acidity for complexity.
- Complementary Flavors: Combine flavors that enhance each other, such as chocolate and raspberry or lemon and vanilla.

2. Layering and Structuring

- Height: Add vertical elements, like a soufflé or a spun sugar decoration, to create visual interest.
- Symmetry and Balance: Arrange components evenly across the plate for a professional look.

3. Plating Composition

- Negative Space: Leave some areas of the plate empty to draw focus to the dessert.

- Focal Point: Design the plate around a central element, such as the main dessert.

4. Precision and Cleanliness

- Clean Lines: Use sharp tools for cutting and ensure no smudges on the plate.

- Uniformity: Ensure all components are consistent in size and shape for a cohesive presentation.

Recipes: Poached Pears, Mille-Feuille, Chocolate Fondant, and Lemon Soufflé

These recipes highlight techniques for creating elegant, restaurant-worthy desserts.

1. Poached Pears

Poached pears are a timeless dessert with a luxurious appearance and a delicate flavor profile.

- Ingredients:
- 4 ripe but firm pears, peeled
- 4 cups water
- 1 1/2 cups sugar
- 1 vanilla bean, split
- 1 cinnamon stick
- Optional: red wine for color and flavor
- Instructions:

1. Combine water, sugar, vanilla bean, and cinnamon in a saucepan. Bring to a simmer.

2. Add pears and cover with parchment paper to submerge them. Poach over low heat for 20–30 minutes until tender.

3. Remove pears and reduce the poaching liquid to a syrup. For a red wine version, replace half the water with wine.

4. Serve pears with a drizzle of syrup and a garnish of fresh mint or a dollop of whipped cream.

2. Mille-Feuille

Also known as a Napoleon, Mille-Feuille is a classic French dessert made with layers of puff pastry and cream.

- Ingredients:
- 1 sheet puff pastry
- 2 cups pastry cream
- Powdered sugar for dusting
- Instructions:

1. Preheat oven to 400°F (200°C). Roll out puff pastry and cut into rectangles. Prick with a fork and bake between two baking sheets to keep flat.
2. Cool the pastry and layer with pastry cream, alternating layers of puff pastry and cream.
3. Dust the top with powdered sugar or drizzle with melted chocolate. Serve with a berry compote for added flavor.

3. Chocolate Fondant

Chocolate fondant, also known as molten lava cake, offers a gooey chocolate center encased in a tender cake.

- Ingredients:
- 4 ounces dark chocolate
- 1/2 cup unsalted butter
- 2 large eggs
- 2 large egg yolks
- 1/4 cup granulated sugar
- 1/4 cup all-purpose flour
- Instructions:

1. Preheat oven to 425°F (220°C). Grease and flour ramekins.
2. Melt chocolate and butter in a double boiler. Cool slightly.
3. Whisk eggs, yolks, and sugar until thick and pale. Fold in the melted chocolate mixture and flour.

4. Pour into ramekins and bake for 10–12 minutes. The edges should be set, but the center should remain soft.

5. Invert onto a plate and serve immediately with ice cream or berry coulis.

4. Lemon Soufflé

A light and airy Lemon Soufflé is an elegant choice that showcases technical skill.

- Ingredients:
- 4 large eggs, separated
- 1/2 cup granulated sugar
- 1/4 cup lemon juice
- Zest of 1 lemon
- 2 tablespoons all-purpose flour
- Butter and sugar for coating ramekins
- Instructions:

1. Preheat oven to 375°F (190°C). Butter and sugar the insides of ramekins.
2. Whisk egg yolks, sugar, lemon juice, zest, and flour until smooth.
3. Beat egg whites to stiff peaks and fold into the lemon mixture.
4. Spoon into ramekins and bake for 12–15 minutes until risen and golden. Serve immediately with powdered sugar or a fruit sauce.

Using Garnishes and Sauces to Elevate Presentation

Garnishes and sauces not only enhance flavor but also transform a dessert into a visual masterpiece.

1. Garnishes

- Edible Flowers: Add elegance and color. Examples include pansies, violets, and nasturtiums.
- Chocolate Decorations: Use tempered chocolate to create curls, shards, or intricate designs.
- Fresh Fruit: Thinly sliced fruits or berries add a natural, vibrant touch.
- Crunchy Elements: Nuts, tuile cookies, or caramel shards provide texture.

2. Sauces

- Fruit Coulis: Blend and strain fresh fruit, then sweeten to taste. Drizzle or create decorative dots and swirls.

- Caramel Sauce: Adds a rich, buttery flavor. Use it to drizzle or pool beneath desserts.

- Chocolate Ganache: Create a luxurious base for desserts or drizzle over the top.

3. Plating Tips

- Precision: Use squeeze bottles or piping bags for clean designs.

- Tools: Use a ring mold for layered desserts or a stencil for powdered sugar patterns.

- Contrast: Pair dark sauces with light desserts for visual impact.

Time Management for Preparing Multiple Components

Plated desserts often involve several elements that need to come together seamlessly. Effective time management is key.

1. Plan Ahead

- Prep Work: Prepare components like pastry cream, sauces, and garnishes in advance.

- Schedule: Break down tasks into manageable steps, allocating time for chilling, baking, and assembly.

2. Staggered Preparation

- Start with Stable Components: Begin with elements that can be made and stored, like pastry layers or poached fruits.

- Finish Fresh: Assemble delicate elements, like soufflés or fondants, just before serving.

3. Use Efficient Tools

- Timers and Thermometers: Avoid overcooking or undercooking with precise timing.

- Organized Workspace: Arrange ingredients and tools to streamline the process.

4. Test Runs

- Practice: Test recipes and plating techniques beforehand to troubleshoot any issues.
- Adjust: Refine flavors, textures, and presentation based on feedback.

Conclusion

Creating elegant plated desserts is a rewarding culinary challenge that combines artistry, precision, and technical skill. By mastering techniques like layering, flavor balancing, and plating composition, and perfecting recipes such as Poached Pears, Mille-Feuille, Chocolate Fondant, and Lemon Soufflé, you can craft showstopping desserts that captivate both the eyes and the palate. With thoughtful use of garnishes and sauces, along with effective time management, you'll be well-equipped to entertain with confidence and flair. Let these desserts transform your gatherings into unforgettable culinary experiences.

Chapter 13: Healthy Desserts: Guilt-Free Indulgence

Desserts are often viewed as indulgent treats, but with the right ingredients and techniques, they can be both delicious and health-conscious. Whether you're catering to dietary restrictions, embracing a healthier lifestyle, or simply exploring new flavors, there's a wide world of guilt-free desserts waiting to be discovered. In this chapter, we'll delve into the art of baking with alternative ingredients like almond flour, coconut milk, and natural sweeteners, and explore gluten-free, vegan, and keto-friendly options. Detailed recipes for Almond Flour Brownies, Vegan Chocolate Mousse, Avocado Ice Cream, and Chia Seed Pudding will showcase how to create healthy, satisfying desserts without compromising on flavor or texture.

Baking with Alternative Ingredients

Traditional baking relies heavily on ingredients like wheat flour, sugar, butter, and cream. In healthy baking, these can be replaced or complemented with alternative options that offer nutritional benefits while catering to specific dietary needs.

1. Gluten-Free Options

For those with gluten sensitivities or celiac disease, gluten-free baking offers a delicious solution.

- Flour Substitutes:
- Almond Flour: Adds moisture, richness, and a mild nutty flavor. Perfect for brownies, cookies, and cakes.
- Coconut Flour: Absorbs liquid well and is ideal for denser desserts.
- Oat Flour: Provides a neutral flavor and a tender texture.
- Tapioca and Arrowroot Starches: Add elasticity and structure.
- Tips for Success:
- Combine multiple gluten-free flours for better texture.

- Use xanthan gum or psyllium husk to mimic gluten's binding properties.

2. Vegan Alternatives

Vegan desserts exclude animal products, relying on plant-based alternatives.

- Egg Substitutes:
- Flaxseed Meal: Mix 1 tablespoon with 3 tablespoons of water to replace one egg.
- Aquafaba: The liquid from canned chickpeas whips up like egg whites.
- Mashed Banana or Applesauce: Adds moisture and sweetness.
- Dairy Substitutes:
- Coconut Milk or Cream: Offers richness and works well in custards and ice creams.
- Almond, Oat, or Soy Milk: Great for cakes and puddings.

3. Keto-Friendly Ingredients

Keto desserts focus on low-carb, high-fat ingredients.

- Flour Alternatives:
- Almond Flour and Coconut Flour: Low in carbs and high in healthy fats.
- Sweeteners:
- Erythritol and Stevia: Zero-carb options that don't spike blood sugar.
- Dairy:
- Full-fat cream and cheese are keto staples for creamy desserts.

4. Natural Sweeteners

Refined sugar can be replaced with natural options that offer added nutrients.

- Honey: Antibacterial properties and a distinct flavor. Best in no-bake desserts and granola.
- Maple Syrup: Rich, caramel-like flavor. Ideal for cookies and cakes.
- Coconut Sugar: Lower glycemic index with a deep, molasses-like taste.
- Dates: Blend into pastes for natural sweetness in brownies and energy bars.

Recipes: Almond Flour Brownies, Vegan Chocolate

Mousse, Avocado Ice Cream, and Chia Seed Pudding

These recipes showcase how alternative ingredients can create decadent, healthy desserts.

1. Almond Flour Brownies

These fudgy brownies are gluten-free, grain-free, and packed with chocolate flavor.

- Ingredients:
- 1 cup almond flour
- 1/3 cup cocoa powder
- 1/2 teaspoon baking powder
- 1/4 teaspoon salt
- 1/2 cup coconut oil or butter, melted
- 3/4 cup coconut sugar
- 2 large eggs
- 1 teaspoon vanilla extract
- 1/2 cup dark chocolate chips
- Instructions:

1. Preheat oven to 350°F (175°C). Grease an 8x8-inch baking pan.
2. Whisk almond flour, cocoa powder, baking powder, and salt in a bowl.
3. In another bowl, mix melted coconut oil, coconut sugar, eggs, and vanilla.
4. Combine wet and dry ingredients, then fold in chocolate chips.
5. Spread batter in the pan and bake for 20–25 minutes. Cool before slicing.

2. Vegan Chocolate Mousse

This mousse is rich and creamy, yet dairy-free and egg-free.

- Ingredients:
- 1 can (14 ounces) full-fat coconut milk, chilled
- 1/2 cup dark chocolate, melted
- 2 tablespoons maple syrup

- 1 teaspoon vanilla extract
- Instructions:

1. Scoop the solid coconut cream from the chilled can into a bowl (save the liquid for smoothies).
2. Whip the coconut cream until fluffy. Fold in melted chocolate, maple syrup, and vanilla.
3. Spoon into serving dishes and chill for at least 2 hours. Garnish with berries or shaved chocolate.

3. Avocado Ice Cream

Creamy avocados make this dessert both healthy and indulgent.

- Ingredients:
- 2 ripe avocados, peeled and pitted
- 1 cup coconut milk
- 1/4 cup honey or maple syrup
- 1 teaspoon vanilla extract
- 1 tablespoon lime juice
- Instructions:

1. Blend avocados, coconut milk, honey, vanilla, and lime juice until smooth.
2. Pour into an ice cream maker and churn according to manufacturer instructions.
3. Freeze for 2–4 hours before serving.

4. Chia Seed Pudding

This nutrient-packed pudding is versatile and easy to prepare.

- Ingredients:
- 1/4 cup chia seeds
- 1 cup almond milk
- 1 tablespoon maple syrup
- 1/2 teaspoon vanilla extract
- Toppings: Fresh fruit, nuts, or granola
- Instructions:

1. Mix chia seeds, almond milk, maple syrup, and vanilla in a jar or bowl.

2. Stir well and refrigerate for at least 4 hours, stirring once after the first hour.

3. Serve with your favorite toppings.

Using Natural Sweeteners Like Honey and Maple Syrup

Natural sweeteners not only reduce refined sugar but also add depth of flavor to desserts.

1. Honey

- Works well in no-bake recipes and marinades.
- Pairs beautifully with citrus, nuts, and yogurt-based desserts.

2. Maple Syrup

- Adds a caramel-like richness to baked goods and frostings.
- Complements flavors like pumpkin, banana, and chocolate.

3. Coconut Sugar

- Ideal for cookies, cakes, and muffins due to its granulated texture.
- Provides a toffee-like flavor, making it perfect for caramel sauces.

Tips for Maintaining Flavor and Texture in Healthy Desserts

Creating healthy desserts that don't compromise on flavor or texture requires thoughtful substitutions and techniques.

1. Enhance Flavors

- Add spices like cinnamon, nutmeg, or cardamom to boost natural sweetness.
- Incorporate citrus zest or vanilla extract for depth.

2. Balance Moisture

- Gluten-free flours often absorb more liquid, so increase the amount of wet ingredients.
- Use applesauce, mashed bananas, or yogurt to retain moisture.

3. Create Texture

- Add crunchy elements like nuts, seeds, or granola for contrast.
- Use whipped aquafaba or coconut cream for light, airy textures.

4. Experiment with Ratios

- Baking with alternative ingredients often requires adjusting proportions. Start small and refine the recipe as needed.
- Combine flours like almond and coconut for better structure.

Conclusion

Healthy desserts prove that indulgence and nutrition can coexist. By embracing alternative ingredients, natural sweeteners, and thoughtful techniques, you can create desserts that cater to diverse dietary needs without sacrificing flavor or texture. Whether it's the rich decadence of Almond Flour Brownies, the creamy allure of Vegan Chocolate Mousse, the refreshing novelty of Avocado Ice Cream, or the wholesome simplicity of Chia Seed Pudding, these recipes and tips offer a guilt-free way to satisfy your sweet tooth. Let these creations inspire your journey into the world of healthy desserts, transforming every treat into a nourishing delight.

Chapter 14: Holiday Treats and Festive Favorites

The holidays are synonymous with indulgence, and desserts often take center stage in festive celebrations. From the warm spices of Christmas treats to the romantic allure of Valentine's Day confections, holiday desserts capture the spirit of the season and bring people together. This chapter explores the art of crafting desserts that embody the essence of each holiday, shares detailed recipes for a Christmas Yule Log, Valentine's Day Red Velvet Cake, Halloween Pumpkin Cookies, and Easter Egg Cheesecake, and offers creative decorating ideas to enhance their festive appeal. Additionally, we'll discuss how to scale recipes for parties and gatherings, ensuring no guest leaves without a taste of sweetness.

Desserts That Capture the Spirit of Each Holiday

Every holiday carries its unique flavor profile and theme, influencing the choice of ingredients, presentation, and decorations.

1. Christmas: Warm and Spiced

Christmas desserts evoke warmth and nostalgia, often featuring spices like cinnamon, nutmeg, and cloves, alongside rich, buttery bases.

- Signature Ingredients:
- Ginger, cinnamon, and nutmeg.
- Chocolate and cream for indulgence.
- Festive elements like cranberries, peppermint, and marzipan.

2. Valentine's Day: Romantic and Decadent

Valentine's Day desserts are all about love and luxury, often incorporating rich flavors and romantic colors like red and pink.

- Signature Ingredients:
- Chocolate in all forms.

- Red fruits like strawberries and raspberries.
- Red velvet and cream cheese for classic charm.

3. Halloween: Fun and Playful

Halloween treats are whimsical and bold, designed to appeal to kids and adults alike with creative designs and autumn-inspired flavors.

- Signature Ingredients:
- Pumpkin and spices like cinnamon and ginger.
- Candy and caramel for indulgence.
- Orange, black, and purple themes.

4. Easter: Bright and Fresh

Easter desserts celebrate renewal and spring, with light, airy flavors and pastel colors.

- Signature Ingredients:
- Lemon, vanilla, and cream.
- Fresh berries and citrus fruits.
- Chocolate eggs and pastel decorations.

Recipes: Christmas Yule Log, Valentine's Day Red Velvet Cake, Halloween Pumpkin Cookies, and Easter Egg Cheesecake

These recipes embody the essence of their respective holidays and are designed to impress.

1. Christmas Yule Log (Bûche de Noël)

A Yule Log is a classic Christmas dessert, featuring a light sponge rolled with cream and decorated to resemble a log.

- Ingredients:
- For the sponge:
- 4 large eggs

- 1/2 cup granulated sugar
- 1/4 cup cocoa powder
- 1/2 cup all-purpose flour
- 1/4 teaspoon salt
- For the filling:
- 1 cup heavy cream
- 2 tablespoons powdered sugar
- 1 teaspoon vanilla extract
- For the frosting:
- 1 cup chocolate ganache or buttercream
- Instructions:

1. Preheat oven to 375°F (190°C). Line a jelly roll pan with parchment paper.
2. Whisk eggs and sugar until pale and fluffy. Sift in cocoa powder, flour, and salt, folding gently to combine.
3. Spread batter evenly in the pan and bake for 10–12 minutes.
4. Turn the sponge onto a clean towel dusted with powdered sugar. Roll up with the towel and cool.
5. Unroll, spread whipped cream, and re-roll. Cover with chocolate frosting and decorate with powdered sugar "snow" and edible holly.

2. Valentine's Day Red Velvet Cake

This rich, red cake symbolizes love and pairs perfectly with cream cheese frosting.

- Ingredients:
- 2 1/2 cups all-purpose flour
- 1/4 cup cocoa powder
- 1 teaspoon baking soda
- 1/2 teaspoon salt
- 1 cup buttermilk
- 1 teaspoon vanilla extract
- 1 teaspoon white vinegar
- 2 tablespoons red food coloring
- 1 cup unsalted butter

- 1 3/4 cups granulated sugar
- 4 large eggs
- For the frosting:
- 8 ounces cream cheese
- 1/2 cup unsalted butter
- 4 cups powdered sugar
- 1 teaspoon vanilla extract
- Instructions:

1. Preheat oven to 350°F (175°C). Grease and flour two 9-inch round pans.
2. Sift together flour, cocoa powder, baking soda, and salt.
3. Cream butter and sugar until light. Add eggs one at a time. Mix in buttermilk, vanilla, vinegar, and food coloring.
4. Gradually add dry ingredients and mix until smooth. Divide between pans and bake for 30–35 minutes.
5. Frost with cream cheese frosting and decorate with heart-shaped sprinkles.

3. Halloween Pumpkin Cookies

Soft and spiced pumpkin cookies with whimsical Halloween decorations.

- Ingredients:
- 2 cups all-purpose flour
- 1 teaspoon baking powder
- 1 teaspoon cinnamon
- 1/2 teaspoon nutmeg
- 1/2 cup unsalted butter
- 1 cup granulated sugar
- 1 large egg
- 1 cup pumpkin puree
- 1 teaspoon vanilla extract
- For the icing:
- 1 cup powdered sugar
- 2–3 tablespoons milk
- Food coloring (orange, black, and green)
- Instructions:

1. Preheat oven to 350°F (175°C). Line baking sheets with parchment paper.

2. Combine flour, baking powder, cinnamon, and nutmeg.

3. Cream butter and sugar until fluffy. Add egg, pumpkin, and vanilla. Gradually mix in dry ingredients.

4. Drop by spoonfuls onto baking sheets and bake for 12–15 minutes.

5. Decorate with icing to create jack-o'-lantern faces or spooky designs.

4. Easter Egg Cheesecake

A creamy cheesecake with colorful Easter egg decorations.

- Ingredients:
- For the crust:
- 1 1/2 cups graham cracker crumbs
- 6 tablespoons melted butter
- For the filling:
- 3 (8-ounce) packages cream cheese, room temperature
- 1 cup granulated sugar
- 3 large eggs
- 1 teaspoon vanilla extract
- Food coloring (pastel shades)
- *For the decorations*:
- Chocolate eggs or pastel candies
- Instructions:

1. Preheat oven to 325°F (160°C). Prepare the crust by mixing crumbs and butter. Press into a springform pan.

2. Beat cream cheese and sugar until smooth. Add eggs one at a time, then vanilla.

3. Divide batter into bowls and tint with pastel food coloring. Drop spoonfuls of each color onto the crust and swirl with a knife.

4. Bake for 50–60 minutes. Cool and chill before decorating with chocolate eggs.

Decorating Ideas for Festive Themes

Decorating transforms a simple dessert into a holiday centerpiece. Here are ideas to match each festive occasion:

Christmas:

- Snowy Effects: Dust powdered sugar over cakes for a snow-like effect.
- Edible Decorations: Use marzipan holly leaves, chocolate pinecones, or sugar snowflakes.

Valentine's Day:

- Romantic Shapes: Cut cookies or cakes into heart shapes.
- Color Palette: Stick to reds, pinks, and whites for icing and decorations.

Halloween:

- Spooky Designs: Use black and orange icing to create bats, pumpkins, or spiderwebs.
- Candy Accents: Incorporate candy eyeballs, licorice, or candy corn.

Easter:

- Pastel Colors: Use light pink, yellow, and green for a springtime vibe.
- Edible Grass: Create "nests" with coconut dyed green for Easter eggs.

How to Scale Recipes for Parties and Gatherings

When hosting a large gathering, scaling recipes effectively ensures everyone gets a taste.

1. Doubling or Tripling Recipes

- Baking Time: Adjust baking times slightly for larger quantities. Keep an eye on doneness.
- Equipment: Use larger pans or multiple baking sheets to accommodate bigger batches.

2. Serving Sizes

- Mini Desserts: Offer smaller portions, like mini cheesecakes or bite-sized cookies, for easy serving.
- Dessert Bars: Create a self-serve station with a variety of treats.

3. Make-Ahead Tips

- Prepare Components Early: Bake cookies, cakes, or crusts a day ahead.
- Assemble Last Minute: Add delicate toppings or frostings just before serving.

Conclusion

Holiday desserts bring joy, tradition, and flavor to festive occasions, making them a cherished part of celebrations. By mastering recipes like the Christmas Yule Log, Valentine's Day Red Velvet Cake, Halloween Pumpkin Cookies, and Easter Egg Cheesecake, and incorporating creative decorating ideas, you can create desserts that not only taste incredible but also look the part. Whether you're hosting a small gathering or a grand party, scaling recipes and preparing ahead ensures your treats are a hit. Embrace the spirit of the holidays and let your desserts be the sweetest highlight of the season!

Chapter 15: Mastering Dessert Presentation and Pairings

Desserts are more than just the final course; they are an opportunity to impress, delight, and create a lasting memory for your guests. Mastering the art of presentation and pairings elevates desserts to a new level, turning them into a visual and sensory masterpiece. This chapter explores the nuances of dessert plating, provides insights into pairing desserts with wines, coffees, and teas, delves into the basics of garnishing, and offers tips for hosting a successful dessert tasting or pairing event.

Plating Techniques: Symmetry, Color, and Texture

Presentation plays a crucial role in the dining experience. A beautifully plated dessert not only enhances its appeal but also sets the tone for indulgence.

1. Symmetry and Balance

- Visual Balance: Arrange elements to create harmony. This doesn't mean everything must be symmetrical, but the composition should feel intentional.

- Rule of Thirds: Divide the plate into thirds and position components at strategic intersections for a dynamic layout.

- Asymmetry: Use asymmetry for a modern look, ensuring each side of the plate complements the other.

2. Color

Color adds visual interest and highlights the dessert's ingredients.

- Contrast: Pair bold colors (e.g., berries) with neutral backgrounds (e.g., white plates).

- Monochrome: Use shades of a single color for elegance, such as a chocolate dessert with cocoa powder, chocolate curls, and ganache.

- Natural Ingredients: Incorporate colorful fruits, herbs, or edible flowers to make the dish vibrant.

3. Texture

Combining different textures creates a multisensory experience.

- Crunchy Elements: Add crushed nuts, brittle, or tuile cookies for contrast.

- Soft and Creamy: Include mousse, whipped cream, or custards for smooth textures.

- Sticky and Chewy: Use caramel, marshmallows, or dried fruits to add complexity.

4. Negative Space

Leaving areas of the plate empty draws attention to the dessert and creates a professional look.

- Minimalist Approach: Let the main component shine by keeping the plate uncluttered.

- Accents: Use drizzles, dollops, or small garnishes to add interest without overwhelming.

5. Tools and Techniques

- Spoons and Brushes: Create swoops, smears, or dollops of sauces for artistic flair.

- Squeeze Bottles: Pipe dots, lines, or intricate designs with precision.

- Ring Molds: Shape layers or stacks for a clean, structured appearance.

Pairing Desserts with Wines, Coffees, and Teas

Pairing desserts with beverages enhances the flavors and overall experience, creating harmony between the food and drink.

1. Wine Pairings

Wine and dessert pairings focus on balancing sweetness, acidity, and richness.

- Sweet Desserts: Match with equally sweet wines like Moscato, Sauternes, or late-harvest Riesling.

- Chocolate Desserts: Pair with rich reds like Port, Banyuls, or a dark Zinfandel.

- Fruity Desserts: Opt for sparkling wines like Prosecco or light whites like Gewürztraminer.

- Nutty Desserts: Pair with sherry, Madeira, or Tokaji.

2. Coffee Pairings

Coffee's robust flavor complements a wide range of desserts.

- Dark Chocolate Desserts: Pair with bold espresso or dark roast.

- Creamy Desserts: Match with lattes or cappuccinos for a smooth contrast.

- Spiced Desserts: Pair with chai-spiced or flavored coffees for complementary notes.

- Fruity Desserts: Choose light or medium roasts to avoid overpowering the flavors.

3. Tea Pairings

Tea's versatility offers endless pairing possibilities.

- Green Tea: Complements citrusy or floral desserts like lemon tarts or matcha cakes.

- Black Tea: Pairs well with spiced or chocolate desserts, such as gingerbread or brownies.

- Herbal Teas: Match fruity tisanes with light desserts like panna cotta or sorbet.

- Oolong Tea: Ideal for creamy or nutty desserts, adding a layer of complexity.

Garnishing Basics: Chocolate Curls, Sugar Work, and Edible Flowers

Garnishes add the finishing touch to a dessert, enhancing its appearance and often its flavor.

1. Chocolate Curls and Shards

Chocolate garnishes add a touch of sophistication.

- Curls:

1. Melt chocolate and spread thinly on a baking sheet.

2. Cool slightly, then scrape with a spatula or knife to create curls.

- Shards:

- Spread melted chocolate thinly, let it set, and break into jagged pieces.

2. Sugar Work

Sugar decorations elevate desserts with their glossy, artistic appeal.

- Caramel Drizzle:

- Heat sugar until amber-colored and drizzle onto parchment paper in decorative patterns. Let cool and set.

- Spun Sugar:

- Dip a fork into molten sugar and flick it back and forth over a rolling pin to create delicate threads.

3. Edible Flowers

Edible flowers provide a natural, colorful garnish.

- Selection: Use flowers like violets, pansies, nasturtiums, or rose petals. Ensure they are pesticide-free.

- Applications: Place whole flowers as accents or press petals onto the sides of cakes.

4. Other Garnishes

- Fresh Fruits: Add slices of kiwi, strawberries, or citrus for a fresh burst of color.

- Herbs: Use mint leaves, basil, or rosemary for a surprising aromatic twist.

- Powders: Dust with cocoa powder, powdered sugar, or matcha for added depth.

Tips for Hosting a Dessert Tasting or Pairing Event

A dessert tasting or pairing event is a memorable way to celebrate flavors, techniques, and creativity.

1. Planning the Menu

- Diverse Selection:

- Include a variety of textures, flavors, and styles (e.g., creamy, crunchy, fruity, chocolatey).

- Seasonality:

- Use seasonal ingredients to ensure freshness and relevance.

2. Setting the Scene

- Themed Decor:

- Match the table setting to the theme, such as elegant for wine pairings or whimsical for a tea party.

- Lighting:

- Use soft lighting to create an intimate atmosphere.

3. Serving Portions

- Tasting Sizes:

- Serve small portions to allow guests to sample multiple desserts without feeling overwhelmed.

- Accompaniments:

- Include palate cleansers like sparkling water or light sorbet between courses.

4. Pairing Guidance

- Provide Notes:

- Offer pairing suggestions for each dessert and beverage.

- Interactive Elements:

- Allow guests to experiment with pairings and share their impressions.

5. Timing and Pacing

- Start Light:

- Begin with lighter desserts and progress to richer, heavier ones.

- Allow Breaks:

- Space out servings to give guests time to savor each pairing.

Conclusion

Mastering dessert presentation and pairings transforms a simple dish into a culinary experience. By perfecting plating techniques, understanding the art of pairing desserts with wines, coffees, and teas, and incorporating garnishes like chocolate curls, sugar work, and edible flowers, you can elevate your desserts to professional standards. Hosting a dessert tasting or pairing event allows you to showcase your creations while offering guests an unforgettable journey through flavors and textures. Let your imagination guide you as you craft desserts that are as beautiful as they are delicious, leaving a lasting impression on everyone who tastes them.

Don't miss out!

Visit the website below and you can sign up to receive emails whenever Olivia Bennett publishes a new book. There's no charge and no obligation.

https://books2read.com/r/B-A-QLEKD-UROAG

BOOKS 2 READ

Connecting independent readers to independent writers.

About the Author

Olivia Bennett is a celebrated food writer and chef with expertise spanning multiple culinary disciplines. With a passion for making home cooking accessible, she specializes in guiding readers through everything from hearty casseroles to delicate pastries. Her work is known for its clear instructions, practical tips, and deep understanding of both traditional and modern cooking techniques.

www.ingramcontent.com/pod-product-compliance
Lightning Source LLC
LaVergne TN
LVHW091117150826
845673LV00002B/872

* 9 7 9 8 2 3 0 0 6 4 0 8 4 *